Maurice Piéron / John Cheffers

Research in Sport Pedagogy

Empirical Analytical Perspective

VERLAG KARL HOFMANN D-7060 SCHORNDORF

CIP-Kurztitelaufnahme der Deutschen Bibliothek

Piéron, Maurice:
Research in sport pedagogy : empir. analyt. perspective /
Maurice Piéron ; John Cheffers. - 1. ed. - Schorndorf :
Hofmann, 1988
  (Sport science studies ; Vol. 2)
  ISBN 3-7780-6421-5
NE: Cheffers, John:; GT

Published as volume 2 of the "Sport Science Studies" series of the International Council of
Sport Science and Physical Education (ICSSPE) with the financial support of UNESCO

Order Number 642

Total production: Karl Hofmann GmbH & Co., D-7060 Schorndorf, Federal Republic of Germany
Printed in Germany · ISBN 3-7780-6421-5

Preface

The International Committee of Sport Pedagogy (ICSP) within the International Council of Sport Science and Physical Education, which has among its members representatives of almost all international associations for physical education, has set out to become a platform for the scientific dialogue of scholars interested in pedagogical research and its transformation into practice.

A first result of the Committee's work is the book on hand. It gives an overview of the empirical-analytical approach within sport pedagogy research. The text is based on the pioneer work of DUNCAN and BIDDLE, which started in the early seventies. Their methodological concept has been particularly fruitful in Western Europe and Northern America, and it appears sensible to present recent research activities and results arising from this concept. The survey merits our interest, although there may be doubts as to whether the empirical-analytical approach is suited to get a grip fully on the complex teaching and learning processes in physical education, and despite the authors limiting themselves primarily to Anglo-American and French source material. The great number of existing scientific approaches clearly indicates that in the long-run the complex structure of reality is only to be analysed by means of a variety of methods. Science, particularly on an international level, is a step-by-step effort directed at gradually focussing in on generally acceptable statements.

It is therefore hoped that representatives of other methodological concepts will also use the forum of the International Committee of Sport Pedagogy in order to share their results with the international confraternity. We trust that a fruitful discussion of different concepts and findings will ensue from such presentations. As a result, we expect to see further changes and more sophisticated models emerge in the not too distant future, and we applaud the efforts of those who bring them about. After all, our research endeavors are expected to help improve the training of our teachers and coaches.

Prof. Dr. AUGUST KIRSCH
President of ICSSPE

We want to express our appreciation to those individuals who have made this text possible. Outstanding typing support was provided by Ida Oriecuia-Cremasco and by Marie-Claire Marchand-Skirole. Thanks are due to Robert Wilmotte for preparing all the figures and to Marc Cloes, Philippe Noël and Ariane Colomberotto (assistants at the University of Liège) for helping in struggling with the draft versions of the manuscript.

M. P.
J. T. C.

Contents

CHAPTER 1

CONCEPTS AND GENERALITIES

It is usual to place artistic and scientific views of teaching at opposite ends of a continuum. This is also true for physical education teaching. So many variables interfere with the teaching process and exert influence on pupil's achievement that studying teaching becomes extremely complex and certainly contingent upon many variables. Teaching remains of humble status from a scientific viewpoint. It is considered by many people as an art necessitating only knowledge and feeling of and for the subject matter. Transmitting knowledge, communicating with the students and providing them with sound practice is considered dependent upon common sense and on inner qualities. We disagree with a totally artistic view of teaching.

There is little doubt that in some part, pedagogy is an art and pedagogical talent can be viewed as stemming from inner powers, however, real artists try to master their art. They base their talent on knowledge and improve their techniques through information and research. Although it may be true that pedagogy is not entirely a science in the restricted sense of the word, Pedagogy is considerably enriched and refined by a multitude of scientific contributions. It is a domain particularly favorable for observation, investigation, and the verification of hypotheses drawn from experiments inside and outside its own field.

Like medicine or other highly qualified professions, education is a practical art and an applied science, a sequence of changing actions designed to reach specific objectives through thoughtful strategies. Pedagogy is a body of theories and rules aimed at guiding teachers and educators in their daily actions. It is multidisciplinary. It deals with aims and objectives, with individuals or with groups, with various means to reach the objectives.

KNOWLEDGE AND COMPETENCIES.

In physical education teaching, all knowledge acquired by the teacher is not necessarily intended to be transmitted to students. A large part of the knowledge acquired by teachers during their professional preparation must be used to select the best strategies to match them with students abilities, skills, and interests. In order to make meaningful interventions, knowing is not enough, it must be translated into doing.

The use of tests, measurements, experiences and systematic observation have allowed us to make predictions and to draw some scientific conclusions about classroom teaching. It is probably the same in physical education.

THE MODEL.

Amongst the many variables influencing teaching, we will concentrate on those which concern the teacher, the conditions in which teaching occurs and the characteristics of those receiving the teaching.

When talking about research in teaching it is common to refer to a model described in the beginning of the sixties by Mitzel (1960), and adapted and modified since by many authors in the domain of classroom teaching (De Landsheere, 1976; Dunkin & Biddle, 1974); Dussault, Leclerc, Brunelle & Turcotte, 1973; Gage, 1972) as well as in physical education (Graham & Heimerer, 1981; Piéron, 1976, 1982a; Tousignant & Brunelle, 1982). This paradigm uses presage, process, product and context variables. The model was designed not only to aid understanding of the teaching process but also to enable research to be summarized.

PRESAGE VARIABLES concern the characteristics of the teacher. They influence the process as well as the outcomes of teaching. For example: formative experience, teaching experience gained in dealing with pupils and classes, personal characteristics such as motivation, intelligence, personality traits, attitudes and values. It could logically be expected that the teaching is under the influence of those in charge of carrying it.

In most research studies dealing with presage variables, "good" teachers have been identified by experts, by supervisors, and by school authorities. Many renowned authors from the classroom teaching research field have pointed out that this kind of research has been disappointing and has provided few results of practical importance for the teacher. According to Bloom (1979), teacher characteristics rarely explain more than 5 % of the variance of student achievement. In many instances, results proved to be lower than these 5 %. Mostly under "Characteristics of the teacher", psychological traits and physical fitness variables have been studied through the use of large, well-validated, but highly suspect descriptive systems, e.g. Cattel's sixteen personality inventory and the AAHPER physical fitness tests. In physical education teaching, results were as poor as in the classroom. It is unfair to base evaluative judgement on the presage and predictive criteria that we have today.

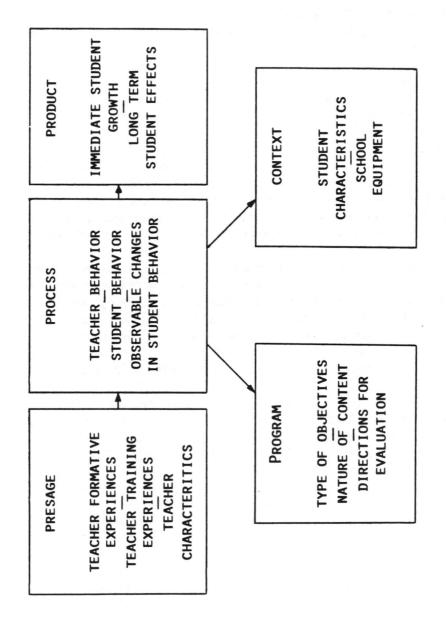

Figure 1.1 – A model for the study of physical education teaching.

PRODUCT VARIABLES concern outcomes of teaching. They must be considered in the short term as well as the long term. Graham & Heimerer (1981) called this activity "The Search for the Perfect Method of Teaching". In this approach, the typical experiment sets out to verify whether students learn more from method A or method B types of learning. Typically, authors involved in these kinds of experiments have labelled their methods as experimental versus traditional, or new versus old, or progressive versus conservative. It is presupposed that in using different methods, teachers will automatically behave differently and that their actual behavior will be in agreement with the characteristics of the defined methods. It is unusual to find a validation of behaviors used during teaching in these experiences. As stated by Flanders (1970):

> "Besides soliciting the cooperation of the teachers, the most difficult problem is to ensure the similarity of teaching within a treatment and to make sure that there are fundamental differences between treatments. Unless the within-group similarities are reasonably consistent and involve identifiable teaching patterns, the intended comparisons may be too weak to permit a fair test of possible differences in the educational outcomes."

In classroom teaching, results of experimental studies based on product measures or on a combination of presage and product variables have usually provided inconclusive results. In physical education, knowledge gathered in this domain remains inconsistant. Comparisons between teaching methods have also provided inconsistent conclusions. It is now time for a more balanced perspective to be adopted in the conduct of research in physical education as opposed to ordinary classroom teaching. When dealing with quantitative objectives more easily measurable than other educational objectives (development of physical fitness, for example), studies centered on product measures have shown that beneficial effects can be expected from physical activities practiced in school physical education. Learning objectives, or educational objectives are less measurable in terms of finite statistics than general fitness.

Concepts and Generalities

Experimental research has failed to substantiate a superior method for teaching physical education, a single, reliable, multipurpose teaching strategy that can be called "The Best Approach". This is not surprising as individual differences among learners are determined by specific interests, needs and abilities.

PROCESS VARIABLES concern the activities and the behaviors occuring in the class, in the gymnasium, on the sports field during teaching periods. The objective aims at identifying what the teacher and the students are doing during the teaching - learning process. We stand here at a crossroad where three series of variables pertaining to those who are delivering the teaching, those who are receiving it, and the conditions in which the teaching is occuring converge.

All those who are using teaching analysis as a research subject have a common preoccupation: to describe the teaching as it is, as it can be observed in real classes, with real pupils and with all the problems of pedagogy and learning and then set about making an appropriate intervention.

CONTEXT VARIABLES concern the teaching environment and the conditions to which the teacher must adjust, more especially with material, equipment, and the general characteristics of the pupils (social environment, age, sex, grade level). Generally, these variables are not directly dependent on the teacher. However, they exert an influence on the quality of teaching. To date, in physical education, most studies have been limited to the investigation of a small number of variables. Sex and grade levels have been the most frequently investigated variables.

PROGRAMME VARIABLES. Tousignant & Brunelle (1982) have made an interesting distinction within context variables in considering separately purely context variables (most of them outside the teacher decision making control) and programme variables related to decision making: type of objectives, nature of content, pedagogical prescriptions or directions for evaluation are examples of these variables.

WHAT IS REALLY GOING ON IN A CLASS ?

In the past, researchers have treated the gymnasium as a black box. Locke (1977) has helped bring this strong picture of "blackbox" from the field of classroom research to physical education. It was assumed that the process events could be ignored without major inconvenience.

Several reasons stress the need for studying the teaching process carefully. An accurate description of any phenomenon is necessary if we are to understand it. That is a common rule for all sciences. They have all passed through a descriptive stage in their development. Lack of accurate instruments to describe or register events can hinder any further development of physical education as a science.

As far as teaching is concerned, description may help identify unusual or exceptional behaviors. Studying the process appears to be a means enabling us to bridge the gap between theory and practice.

Two other reasons seem to be of special importance: the lack of an accurate perception of what is going on in the class and the variability of teaching behaviors.

It has been pointed out that teachers have not been aware of the plurality of behaviors in the classroom, and this lack of awareness at times interferes with their effectiveness. According to Good & Brophy (1978), this problem exists for at least three basic reasons: (1) teacher training programs spend little time training teachers to perform specific behavior or to describe specific teaching behavior; (2) classrooms are busy places, and teachers are so busy responding that they have little time to think about what they are doing; (3) teachers are seldom observed on any systematic basis so that they seldom get valuable information about ways to increase their effectiveness.

In classroom teaching research, evidence has shown that classroom teachers misinterpret their own teaching behaviors and that teachers themselves were unable to describe accurately even simple classroom behaviors such as percentages of time that they or their students spent in talking. In data reported by Good &

Brophy (1978) most teachers grossly underestimated the amount of time they talked. The teachers could not accurately describe what they did in the classroom.

In physical education, studies comparing the perceived and the actual interactions or teacher behaviors emphasized that teachers encountered great difficulty in meeting their predicted behaviors. They generally saw themselves closer to education theories than they actually were. Nygaard (1978) observed that there were no significant differences between experienced teachers and inexperienced teachers in their predicted behaviors. Their predicted behaviors were not substantiated by their recorded behaviors. Batchelder (1975) compared predicted estimates of teacher behaviors as reflected by seventeen parameters of CAFIAS. Significant differences ($p < .01$) were found between estimated and observed behaviors in 88 % of the parameters.

Other important elements of teaching are badly perceived by teachers. Telama, Paukku, Varstala & Paananen (1982) reported several significant differences between teachers and students in assessing the effects of physical education lessons, in assessing the physical stress or the enjoyement experienced in physical education lessons.

The inter-individual variability distribution in teaching is large (Anderson & Barrette, 1978b). Frequently the standard deviation is higher than the mean. On the other hand, the intra-individual variability seems to be low. Considerable differences between teachers have been observed in using the same type of behavior. For example, feedback has been observed to occur at a rate of four to five behaviors per minute (Brunelle & de Carufel, 1982; Piéron & R. Delmelle, 1981). These behaviors occurred at a rate of once per minute in other physical education research although careful distinction must be made of the kind of feedback experienced (Arena, 1979; Fishman & Tobey, 1978). In general, all research has determined that most feedback is of a relatively unimportant nature with little prescriptive advice or assistance.

The intra-individual variability can be another source of concern. Conflicting results emerge from the research on teacher behavior and interaction analysis. Lombardo (1979) observed the teacher - pupil interaction of four teachers, twice a day, for 20 days, and concluded that variables of time of day, grade level, and day of week had negligible influence on the teacher behaviors and interaction patterns in physical education classes. The same teachers reobserved two years later used the same behaviors and patterns of teaching for two thirds of the time under careful scrutiny (Lombardo, 1982). As pointed out by Lombardo & Cheffers (1983), the variable of lesson content seems to exert considerably greater influence on teacher behavior than with the student credibility.

Demarteau and Piéron (1978) observed the same teacher during nine lessons and found that the Kendall coefficient of concordance between categories amounted to .82, reflecting an overall stability of the teacher's behaviors. In student teachers, the same coefficient was found to amount to .95 (Piéron, 1978b).

This view of teaching behavior variability is partly confirmed by Rink (1983). Three teachers were observed over a fifteen lesson volleyball unit. The observation system used, Observation System for Content Development - Physical Education (OSCD-PE) differs largely from the CAFIAS used by Lombardo (1979) or by Lombardo & Cheffers (1983).

The stability of instructional behaviors was determined by the range and standard deviation for each teacher over the unit. Rink (1983) described three evolutionary trends for teaching behaviors:

(1) Stable behaviors remaining at the same level throughout the whole teaching unit; that is the case for organization functions both for management of the class or student behavior control. The specificity of teacher feedback remained relatively stable through the unit. Refining behavior was a relatively stable behavior with a decrease toward the end of the unit when emphasis was put on game playing.

(2) Unstable behaviors with any apparent relationship with the position within the teaching unit, lesson beginning time, and communication of content.

(3) Behaviors tending to change in the same direction over the unit: allocated time for practice increased from beginning to

end. This trend was not completely explained by increased game-like play. The use of questionning decreased as the teaching unit progressed.

OBSERVATION OF TEACHERS.

The study of the teaching process uses systematic observation as the main tool to gather data. According to Simon & Boyer (1970), there are three prerequisites for any observation analysis system. It must be descriptive rather than evaluative, must deal with what can be measured and categorized and must deal with small behaviors or acts rather than with huge concepts.

Cheffers (1978) distributed current systems under two broad headings:

(1) Inductive, where the systems materialize and attain form only after a series of observations have been made. Examples are anecdotal recording, critical incidents, dialogue analysis, ethnographic observational data;

(2) Deductive, where a formula pre-exists and interpretations are made through that formula. Most deductive systems develop as a result of the inductive process.

No single system can describe the complexity of teaching. The best that can be expected is a partial picture of the reality of classrooms or gymnasia.

Devising an observation system starts by carefully defining the behaviors or events to be recorded. Examples and specific rules of coding are used to illustrate the categorization.

Each time an instrument is developed, it should be tested for validity and inter- and intra-observer reliability.

Validity : Measures of face, content, and construct validity are necessary. Face validity refers to the need to show that the instrument is somewhere on target with its goals and objectives when compared with non-relevant instrumentation. Content validity is concerned with the relevance of the categories to the content area adressed, and is mostly confirmed through literature research, interaction amongst specialists in the relevant field, and through cognitive debate. Construct validity is the most important validation process. It is concerned with whether the new instrument adequately measures and/or predicts the traits or meanings when compared with other similar instruments measuring the same general constructs. Obviously, construct validation procedures project specific instrument refinement techniques, and safeguards against unnecessary and redundant instrument proliferation.

Reliability : For an instrument to be reliable, it must produce the same data in replicated situations. Of great significance is the ability of the observer to recognize the same categories under replication, and to be in reasonable agreement with another observer independently administering the same instrument. Measures of reliability are confirmed by correlational and variance techniques. Different methods exist to assess the reliability. Their utilization could be dependent on the unit of observation used.

Although it cannot be clearly affirmed that there is no observer effect, it seems that it should be kept to a minimum. In classroom teaching observation, Samph (1968) undertook a study to determine whether the presence of an observer has an effect on the verbal behavior of teachers and if so, what the nature of that effect is. The Flanders Interaction Analysis System (FIAS) was used to code the recorded teacher verbal behaviors. Analysis of the data demonstrated the existence of a small observer effect. Teachers became more "indirect" when an observer was present in their classroom, whether they were informed of an observation prior its occurance or not. The teachers in this study used more "praise", "acceptance of ideas" and less "criticism" when being observed (Samph, 1968). Dealing with the observed effect in the Video Data Bank study, Anderson (1978) concluded: "Although we cannot claim that our presence had no effect on what transpired, the apparent effect was minimal. In fact, with few exceptions the videotaped classes closely resembled other casually observed classes taking place in the same school".

Concepts and Generalities

Units of observation: Different observation units can be used: event recording, time sampling, interval recording, duration recording.

"In event recording one tally is marked for each occurence of a previously defined behavior within the observation interval. Tallying the number of baskets made by a guard in a basketball scrimmage, marking the number of "good" tennis serves by Player X in a match, or recording the number of times Team Z throws incomplete passes during a college football game are examples of event recording.

In time sampling, brief intervals within the observation period are marked off and the defined behavior is observed at the very end of each brief interval and then recorded as either occurring or not occuring at that time. Looking up every ten seconds to see if Player A is handling the ball during a soccer game, checking every fifteen minutes to determine whether or not a group of children is arguing, or watching at the end of thirty-second intervals to find out if a student is working on programmed instruction modules are all examples of time sampling.

Interval recording is very similar to time sampling, except that observation is done during each brief interval instead of just at the end of each one. A defined behavior need occur only once during the brief interval to be recorded as present, and even if it occurs many times, only one tally is recorded. Checking to see if an athlete is watching a loop film, if he is practicing his golf swing, or if he is retrieving golf balls already hit could all be observed by interval recording.

Duration recording is used when the length of time a defined behavior lasts is the important item in the observation. How long a teacher lectures, how long the students take to organize into teams after being asked to do so, how long it takes rollcall are illustrations of behaviors that could duration recorded. This technique is generally recorded as elapsed minutes and seconds ..." (Dodds, 1978).

ANALYZING THE TEACHING OF PHYSICAL EDUCATION.

The first studies dealing with teacher behavior or with teacher - pupil interaction occured during the late sixties (Barrett, 1969; Bookhout, 1966, 1967). The first specific systems of observation for physical education were devised during the same period (Barrett, 1971; Fishman & Anderson, 1971). In physical education, Anderson (1971) was probably the first to focus our attention to the potential of descriptive analytic research.

This area of study remained confined to a few universities in North America for several years, before a strong and growing interest developed at a broader international level. In July 1976, international endeavours materialized approximately at the same time in two international congresses: in Jyvaskyla (Finland) and in Quebec City (Canada). At the Jyvaskyla congress, "Evaluation" was set forth as the general theme and a special section was devoted to teacher evaluation. Several papers dealt with teacher - pupil interaction. In Quebec City, the preolympic congress (CISAP) included a section entitled "Pedagogy of Sports". Two introductory reports concerned the topic of teachers behavior and interaction with students (Brunelle, 1978; Piéron, 1978a). Several papers provided data on teacher and sports instructor behaviors and on teacher student interaction. Batchelder & Cheffers (1978) presented the nature and validation procedures of the instrument CAFIAS at this Conference along with preliminary research findings.

Since then, seminars and congresses featuring these topics have multiplied, especially under the leadership of AIESEP (Association Internationale des Ecoles Supérieures d'Education Physique) in Madrid (1977), Macolin (1978), Rio de Janeiro (1981), Boston (1982), Jyvaskyla (1982), Rome (1983), the Olympic Scientific Congress in Eugene, Oregon (1984), and at Adelphi University, Long Island (1985). Other congresses or workshops have dealt with the same topic, systematic teaching observation in physical education, in Kiel (ICHPER, 1979), Columbus (Ohio State University, 1982), West Lafayette (Purdue University, 1982).

In spite of its fast development, the topic remains still restricted. Papers appear more frequently in professional and in research journals, but are relatively rare when compared to other field, of publications in physical education research. This must be considered an impediment to the development of the field. The recent publication of the Journal of Teaching in Physical Education meets an urgent need and tends to fill a real gap in this domain.

Documents reviewed here have been selected according to these relatively strict criteria and ready availability. Three kinds of documents have been reviewed:

* papers published in journals or in congress proceedings;

* doctoral dissertations available through microfilm and microfiche services;

* research reports available from the universities or centers sponsoring the research.

Two types of documents were discarded because of their unequal quality and lack of availability:

* master theses;

* unpublished papers delivered in national conventions.

The more elegant of these papers deserve to be refined and published. Reference to these papers can only be regarded as limited due to the registered differences in the base line criteria and the use of to many of this type of reference tends to decrease the credibility of research in the field of pedagogy.

Gage (1968) proposed that research on teaching occurs when teacher behaviors serve as independent variables and some measure of pupil learning as the dependent variables. Locke used this proposal to define the field: "Research on teaching physical education includes only studies which employ data gathered through direct or indirect observation of instructional activity" (Locke, 1977).

To present the research related to teaching in physical education, we used an adaptation of the format of Dunkin and Biddle (1974) as a model:

* studies reviewed;

* instrument, method of gathering data, design of studies, subjects, context;

* comparison according to context and programme variables.

As in Dunkin & Biddle's book (1974), each study is assigned an acronym and indicated in parentheses, which is used to indicate design features. Methodology of research deals with different kinds of design features that are associated with the instrument, the method of gathering data, the subjects observed, the design of the study, the subject matter taught and the context. Due to the diversity of methodologies used in the studies reviewed, it was sometimes impossible to stay strictly within the confines of the model.

Let us take two examples:

In box 2.1, the reader will find:

Anderson & Barrette (1980)   (A&B80)

It refers to Anderson & Barrette (1980). Teacher behavior in physical education classes. In, G. Schilling & W. Baur (Eds), Audiovisuelle Medien im Sport. Moyens audiovisuels dans le sport. Audiovisual means in sports, Basel, Birkhauser Verlag, 255-276.

In box 2.2, the reader will find:

(A&B,80)   20 Cl (elem), 20 Cl (second), 40 T, videotapes
              Various subject matters
              School level, Cl segment

This means that in the Anderson & Barrette publication, 20 classes at the elementary level, 20 classes at the secondary level directed by 40 teachers were videotaped. Lessons dealt with different subject matter. Data were compared according to school level and class segment.

Concepts and Generalities

In box 4.1, the reader will find:

Piéron & Haan (1980)   (P&H80)

It refers to Piéron, M. & Haan, J.M. (1980) Pupils activities, time on task and behaviours in high school physical education teaching. Bulletin of the Fédération Internationale d'Education Physique, 50, 3/4, 62-68.

In box 4.2, the reader will find:

(P&H,80)   300 S, JHS, T, live, OBEL/ULg,
              Team sports, Track and field, Gymnastics
              Subject matter, Gender & coed

Three hundred students at the junior high school level have
been observed by means of the OBEL/ULg observation system.
Number of teachers was not mentionned the study. Students were
observed during team sports, track and field, and gymnastics
classes. Data were compared according to the subject matter
taught, the student gender, and in coeducational classes.

In the text, various figures, percentages, and intervention
rates have been quoted. The reader must be fully aware that they
are only of indicative value. Authors have used different observational units (event recording, time sampling, interval recording, duration recording). Categories drawn from the same concepts or teaching functions are not always defined exactly in the
same way. Some overlapping may occur. It would be hazardous to
compare these figures too literally.

ABREVIATIONS.

C   Coach
CBTE   Competency Based Teacher Education
Cl   Class
Cont   Control
CT   Cooperating Teacher
Elem   Elementary level
ETU   Experimental Teaching Unit

Exp   Experimental
F   Female
Gr   Grade
IA   Interaction Analysis
JHS   Junior High School
Less   Lesson
M   Man, Male
MET   Motor Engagement Time
MT   Master Teacher
Obs   Observer
PE   Physical Education
Pl   Player
S   Student
Sec   Secondary level
SHS   Senior High School
Sup   Supervisor
ST   Student Teacher
T   Teacher
TSRT   Teaching Situation Reaction Test
Univ   University level
W   Women

OBSERVATION SYSTEMS.

ALT-PE   Academic Learning Time - Physical Education
BESTPED   Behavior of Students in Physical Education
CBAS   Coaching Behavior Assessment System
CAFIAS   Cheffers Adaptation of Flanders Interaction Analysis
           System
DAC   Dyadic Adaptation of CAFIAS
DACOME   Data Collection for Managerial Efficiency in Physical
           Education
DAOS   Dalhousie Athlete Observation Schedule
DCOS   Dalhousie Coach Observation Schedule
FEED/ULg   Feedback / Université de Liège (Feedback / University
           of Liège)
FIAS   Flanders Interaction Analysis System
FOTOP   Flow of Teacher Organizational Patterns
IRG   Individual Reaction Gestalt
ITBAS   Individualized Teacher Behavior Analysis System
IVI-PE   Implicit Value Instrument for Physical Education

LoCoBAS	Lombardo Coaching Behavior Analysis System
OBEL/ULg	Observation de l'élève / Université de Liège (Student Observation / University of Liège)
ORRPETB	Observational Recording Record of Physical Educator's Teaching Behavior
OScAR	Observation Schedule and Record
OSCD-PE	Observation System for Content Development - Physical Education
OSIA-PE	Observational System for Instructional Analysis - Physical Education
PEIAC	Physical Education Interaction Analysis Categories
PETGAS	Physical Education Teacher Guidance Analysis Schedule
PETAI	Physical Education Teacher Assessment Instrument
PROF/ULg	Professeur / Université de Liège (Teacher / University of Liège)
RIAS	Rankin Interaction Analysis System
SCOL	Systematic Coaching Observation by Lucas
STOP	Student Teachers Observing Peers
TBOS	Teacher Behavior Observation System
TRI-LASP	Teacher's Role in Learning Activity Selection Process
TRIPAC	Teacher's Role in Providing Activity Choice

CHAPTER 2

TEACHER BEHAVIOR

There has always been a controversy between teacher centered and student centered teaching. A balance between both approches is probably the more desirable of either alternative. If the teacher tries to transfer some part of the decision making process to the student, this must be envisaged as a carefully planned move. The decision making process relies on education too. All students will not progress at identical rates. In the last resort, teachers are accountable for what is happening in a class and are the primary decision makers. Tasks on which pupils have to spend time are defined and identified mostly by teachers. To the extent that they do not function as decision makers, they will be controlled by class events. When they cannot control these events, progress is often poor for most of the pupils. Therefore it is understandable that a large part of studies aiming at a better knowledge of physical education classes behaviors started by focusing on teachers'behaviors.

Some data from the classroom teaching research showed that the converse of teacher-centered, student choice of activities, can yield negative results. Classrooms that are organized so that students have a great deal of choice are usually ones with lower academic engaged time and lower achievement. For example, in the study by Soar (1973), student free choice, student limited choice, and free work groups were associated with lessened academic achievement. For Stalling & Kaskowitz (1974), child selection of seating and work groups yielded similar, consistent negative correlations with achievement. These two studies were limited to children of low socioeconomic status backgrounds. However, Solomon & Kendall (1976) obtained the same results in their study of children in 30 fourth-grade suburban classrooms. In this study, classrooms in which students chose their own activities and followed their own interests, were responsible for class planning (and were not teacher - dependent) were also the classrooms characterized by rowdiness, shouting, noise, and disorderliness (Rosenshine, 1978).

When looking at the teacher's behavior, it is understandable that on the early emphasis was put on verbal behaviors. Verbal communication is the first and most used channel in teaching. However the non verbal communication channel is considered to be particularly important for physical education teaching as it supplements, reinforces and modifies the verbal message. Dissa-

tisfied with data provided by the solely verbal behaviors, several authors tried to account better for the non verbal events in
their analysis (Cheffers, 1973; Mancuso, 1972).

Two options were open to observers in describing what happening during a teaching period: to use existing observation
systems or to use specific, newly devised systems. The use of
existing systems is viewed from the perspective that physical
education is one of all general educational subject matters and
attempting to achieve general educational objectives besides its
specific aims. Studies purport to answer questions such as: How
well does physical education fulfill educational aims? How much
does physical education differ from other subject matters? Studies using the Cheffers Adaptation of Flanders Interaction Analysis System (CAFIAS) are the best example of this trend (Cheffers,
Mancini & Martinek, 1980). The development of original observation systems demonstrates an intent to account for the specific
nature of physical education teaching, its specific structure of
performance and its variety of environments. The Video Data Bank
Project developed under the leadership of Anderson at Teachers
College, Columbia University represents a good example of this
tendency (Anderson, 1971, 1975 ; Anderson & Barrette, 1978b).

Observational studies of teachers'behavior can be categorized into two groups: (1) description of a comprehensive profile
of teacher interventions and behaviors; (2) multidimensional
analysis of specific interventions supposed to be essential in
the teaching process or to facilitate the motor skill development.

Box 2.1 - Teacher's Behaviors: Studies and Papers reviewed

Anderson & Barrette (1978b)   (A&B78b)
Anderson & Barrette (1980)   (A&B80)
Anderson (1983)   *(And83)
Arena (1979)   (Are79)
Armstrong (1977)   (Arm77)
Armstrong & Hoffman (1979)   (A&H79)

Bailey (1982)   *(Bail82)
Bain (1974)   (Bai74)
Bain (1976a)   (Bai76a)
Bain (1976b)   (Bai76b)
Bain (1978)   (Bai78)
Bain (1983b)   *(Bai83b)
Barrett (1969)   (Barr69)
Barrett (1971)   *(Barr71)
Barrette (1977)   (Bar77)
Bochman, Heiduk & Ullrich (1975)   (B,H&U 75)
Bressane (1982)   (Bre82)
Brunelle (1973)   (Bru73)
Brunelle (1975)   (Bru75)
Brunelle & de Carufel (1982)   (B&C82)
Brunelle et al. (1983)   (Bru83)
Carlier & Andreani (1980)   (C&A80)
Caruso (1980)   (Car80)
Catelli (1979)   (Cat79)
Cole (1979)   (Col79)
Demarteau & Pieron (1978)   (D&P78)
Devlin, Mancini & Frye (1981)   (D,M,F81)
Dodds (1983)   *(Dod83)
Erbani (1982)   (Erb82)
Faria Junior (1980)   (Far80)
Fishman & Anderson (1971)   *(F&A71)
Fishman (1974)   (Fis74)
Fishman & Tobey (1978)   (F&T78)
Freedman (1978)   (Fre78)
Gustart (1985)   (Gus85)
Harrington (1974)   (Har74)
Hughley (1983)   *(Hug83)
Hupe (1974)   (Hup74)
Hurwitz (1974)   (Hur74)
Hurwitz (1983)   *(Hur83)
Johnson (1983)   *(Joh83)
Levison (1978)   (Lev78)
Lewis (1983)   *(Lew83)
Lucas (1978b)   (Luc78b)
Martinek & Karper (1982)   (M&K82)
Mawer & Brown (1982)   (M&B82)
Morgenegg (1983)   (Mor83)
Oien (1979)   (Oie79)

Olson (1983a)   *(Ols83a)
Ospelt & Schilling (1978)   (O&S78)
Petersen (1980)   (Pet80)
Philipps & Carlisle (1983a)   *(P&C83a)
Piéron (1978)   (Pie78)
Piéron & Hacourt (1979)   (P&H79)
Piéron & Devillers (1980)   (P&D80)
Piéron (1980)   (Pie80)
Piéron (1982a)   (Pie82a)
Piéron & R. Delmelle (1981)   (P&D81)
Piéron & R. Delmelle (1982)   (P&D82)
Piéron & V. Delmelle (1983)   (P&VD83)
Piéron & Georis (1983)   (P&G83)
Piéron, Neto & Carreiro da Costa (1985) (P,N,C85)
Quarterman (1978)   (Qua78)
Quarterman (1983)   *(Qua83)
Rehbein (1981)   *(Reh81)
Rink (1979)   (Rin79)
Rink (1983)   (Rin83)
Rushall & Richards (1981)   (R&R81)
Showers (1974)   (Sho74)
Siedentop & Rife (1983)   *(S&R83)
Stewart (1977)   (Ste77)
Stewart (1983)   *(Ste83)
Tobey (1977)   (Tob77)
Twa (1979)   (Twa79)
Varstala, Telama & Akkaken (1981)   (V,T,A81)
Varstala, Paukku & Telama (1983)   (V,T,P83)
Vendien (1981)   *(Ven81)
Westcott (1977)   (Wes77)
Yokoyama (1981)   (Yok81)
Zakrajzek (1983)   *(Zak83)

* Papers dealing only with the description of instruments

INSTRUMENTS FOR OBSERVATION.

Several instruments have been developed to focus on teacher's interventions. They provide a quantitative distribution of the events.

Box 2.2 - Profile of Teachers'behaviors: Instruments of observation & Methods of gathering data.

INSTRUMENTS:

(Bai,76b) Implicit values instrument for physical
(Bai,74)   education (IVI-PE)
           T behaviors, Cl organisation, procedural regulations
           12 T (6M, 6W), 3 Less per T
           Team sports
           Reliability (two-way ANOVA)

(Barr,69) 5 Obs, 12 Less, *(Barr71)
           low to moderate inter- and intra-reliability
           Multidimensional, movement tasks, content,
           guidance, student response

(Far,80)   FaMOC
           35 Obs, audio & video
           Animation & Instruction
           Description, validity, reliability

(Hup,74)   Adaptation of Bellack, Openshaw & Cyphert
           Dimensions: sign, function, substantive,
           logical, instructional
           4 Obs, video and simulated live observation
           High reliability (video) to low reliability
           (simulated live observation)

(Hur,74)   T's Role in Learning Activity Selection
            Process (TRI-LASP)
            T's role: director, predictor, identifier,
            encourager, no role
            Video, content validity, high reliability

(Sho,74)   3 Obs, 5 T, 9 experts
            Various subject matters
            Description, reliability, validity
            Categories: Clarity & knowledge of subject,
            friendliness & interests in students,
            enthusiasm & sense of humor, fairness

---

(1) The system used by Anderson & Barrette (1978b, 1980)
includes dimensions allowing to describe four different aspects
of each intervention: interactive function (see table 2.1), subscripts indicating the extent to which the teacher carries out the
function, shares it or delegates it to students. The communication function indicates how the teacher interacts with others
(talking, listening, observing, using student demonstrator ...,
participating). The direction identified the other person(s)
toward whom the teacher's behavior is conveyed: one student,
groups, ... the whole class.

(2) Behavioral categories used in the instrument devised by
Stewart (1977, 1983) "Observational Recording Record of Physical
Educator's Teaching Behavior" (ORRPTEB) were selected from other
systems namely CAFIAS (Cheffers, 1973), OSU rating scale
(Hughley, 1983), and Tharp & Gallimore (1976). A total of 27
teacher behaviors categories, four student categories referred to
as climates and five teacher - student interaction categories in
the system. The observation schedule used by Freedman (1978) in
comparing teachers and student teachers was very close to the
instrument used by Stewart (1977).

(3) Piéron (1978a, 1978b), Demarteau & Piéron (1978), Piéron
(1982a) started from a general system (De Landsheere & Bayer,
1974) to select main categories dealing with content, management,

feedback, affectivity, and silent observation. Sub-categories were devised for specific use in physical education. Student verbal intervention is accounted for in the system.

Table 2.1 - Dimensions and categories of teacher behaviors (Anderson & Barrette, 1978).

Dimension: INTERACTIVE FUNCTION - Identifies the purpose of teacher's interactive behavior

1. Preparing for Motor Activities
   1.1 Organizing
   1.2 Preparatory Instructing
   1.3 Providing Equipment or Readying the Environment

2. Guiding the Performance of Motor Activities
   2.1 Concurrent Instructing
   2.2 Officiating
   2.3 Spotting
   2.4 Leading Exercises
   2.5 Intervening Instruction

3. Observing the Performance of Motor Activities

4. Participating in Motor Activities

5. Other Interacting Related to Motor Activities

6. Other Interactive Behaviors
   6.1 Administering
   6.2 Establishing and Enforcing Codes of Behavior
   6.3 Other Interacting

7. Non-Interactive Intervals
   7.1 Dealing with Equipment
   7.2 Other Non-Interactive Behaviors

8. Non-Discernable Behaviors
   8.1 Insufficient Audio-Video
   8.2 Absent from Gymnasium

Dimension: FUNCTION SUBSCRIPTS - Indicates the extent to which the teacher carries out the function himself/ herself, or shares it with others

1. Does
2. Shares
3. Delegates

Dimension: MODE - Identifies the way(s) in which the teacher interacts with others, i.e. the ways in which he/ she conveys messages to others, receives messages from others or acts upon them

1. Talks
2. Listens
3. Observes
4. Demonstrates
5. Uses Student Demonstrator
6. Uses Audio-Visual Aids
7. Uses Signaling Devices
8. Writes or Provides Written Materials
9. Manually Assists
10. Participates
11. Perform Physical Task

Dimension : DIRECTION - Identifies the other person(s) toward whom the teacher's behavior is directed

1. One Student
2. Group / Whole Class of Students
3. One Student and Group / Whole Class
4. Other Persons (other than Enrolled Students)
5. Other Combinations (of above)

---

(4) Rink (1979) developed an instrument to gather information on two major instructional events: instructional behavior and the specific arrangements of the instructional setting. Categories were developed around the concepts of contribution to content development, communication function, design function, recipient / characteristics of the source, activity time, negative expressions, student verbal behaviors. The reliability ranged from low to high according to these functions.

(5) Mawer & Brown (1982), devised the Physical Education Teacher Guidance Analysis Schedule (PETGAS) with a main focus to the guidance behavior of the teacher. The system has six dimen-

sions, (rejecting, focusing, accepting, questionning, organising, unrelated statements) and a total of 21 different categories.

(6) The system developed by Bailey (1982) identifies the managerial and teaching functions as key dimensions to study teacher behaviors. The system consisted of four dimensions and 19 categories. Unfortunately, descriptive data have not been provided to date.

(7) The Physical Education Teacher Assessment Instrument (PETAI) is an instrument which deals equally with teacher and student behavior: three categories for each. Phillips & Carlisle (1983a) based their model on several research data (BTES, ALT, CAFIAS) to build their model. Teacher behavior is observed under three broad categories: analyzing students needs (awareness of skill level, knowledge of content, objectives, utilization of testing, flexibility and appropriateness of instruction), instruction time (planned instruction, response presentation, observation, questionning, positive feedback, negative feedback), management time (beginning class, recording tasks, equipment management, organization, behavioral feedback, ending class). Student behavior is also distributed in three categories: student allocated skill learning time (warm-up activities, engaged skill learning, success time during engaged skill learning, non-engaged skill learning, engaged game playing, success time in engaged game playing, non-engaged game playing), student management time (same sub-categories than for teacher), and student achievement. This assessment system was used in a teacher effectiveness study (see chapter 5).

Several other observation systems have been described in "Systematic Observation Instrumentation for Physical Education" (Darst, Mancini & Zakrajsek, 1983) : "OSU Teacher Behavior Rating Scale" (Hughley, 1983), "Data Collection for Managerial Efficiency in Physical Education (DACOME)" (Siedentop & Rife, 1983), "Student Teachers Observing Peers (STOP)" (Dodds, 1983), "Observational Recording Record of Physical Educator's Teaching Behavior (ORRPETB)" (Stewart, 1983), "Teacher's Role in Providing Activity Choice (TRIPAC)" (Hurwitz, 1983), "Flow of Teacher Organizational Patterns (FOTOP)" (Johnson, 1983), "Physical Education Teacher / Coach Observational System" (Quarterman, 1983), "Teacher / Coach and Pupil Athlete Observation Schedules"

(Rushall, 1983), "Implicit Values Instrument for Physical Education (IVI-PE)" (Bain, 1983b).

BEHAVIOR PROFILE OF PHYSICAL EDUCATION TEACHERS.

A general profile of teacher interventions can be described as instruction or presentation of content, augmented feedback, organization or management, silent observation of students, affectivity. Verbal interventions from students can be used to shift from a profile of teacher's intervention to a profile of interaction. The quantitative part of these behaviors varies according to several contextual or programme variables. They will be discussed later.

Box 2.3 - FIELD STUDIES: Design of studies, methods of gathering data, contexts.

(A&B,78)	20 Cl (elem), 20 Cl (second), 40 T, video
(A&B,80)	Various subject matters
(Bar,77)	School level, Cl segment
(Bai,76a)	12 T (6 M, 6 W), second, IVI-PE
	Team sports
	Gender, environment (urban, suburban)
(Bai,78)	20 T (10 M, 10 W), 20 C, IVI-PE
	Various subject matters
	Gender, situation (teaching - coaching)
(B,H,U,75)	42 & 30 Less, Verbal behaviors
	Descriptive study
(Bre,82)	1 ST, audio, FaMOC
	Descriptive study
(Bru,73)	5 ST, audio, Joyce system
	Descriptive and case study

(C&A,80)   3 groups (subjects = ?), Joyce System
             Comparison of teaching styles

(D,M,F,81)   4 T, 40 S (disruptive), DAC
             Martinek & Zaichkovsky self concept scale
             Exp (instruction in contingency management
             skills) vs Cont groups

(D&P,78)   1 T (9 Cl), Video, De Landsheere & Bayer observation
             system
             Various subject matters
             Intra-individual variability, Descriptive

(Erb,82)   22 ST (12M, 10 W), Specific instrument
             Various subject matters (mostly team sports)
             Comparison according to previous sports experience.

(Fre,78)   14 T, 16 St, elem, second, live
             School level, teaching experience

(Gus,85)   3 T (M), 10 Less, audio, OSCD-PE
             Volleyball unit
             Intra-individual variability

(Luc,78b)   16 T, 42 Less, gr 6 to 12, Florida
             taxonomy of cognitive behavior
             Various subject matters
             "Conceptual" vs "Traditional" approach

(M&B,82)   20 T (11 M, 9 W), 60 Cl, elem, PETGAS
             Gymnastics
             Gender

(Oie,79)   5 ST, 10 Cl, 316 S, JHS, ITBAS
             T perception of S performance, T perception of
             S in Cl
             personality

(Pie,78)   15 ST, microteaching, video, De Landsheere & Bayer
             observation System
             Team sports
             Relationships between verbal and non verbal behaviors

(P&H,79)   24 T (10 M, 14 W), elem, JHS, SHS, live,
           De Landsheere & Bayer observation System
           Various subject matters
           Gender, grade level

(Pie,82)   12 M, 10 ST, JHS, SHS, PROF/ULg
           Volleyball, Gymnastics
           Teaching experience, subject matter, school level

(Rin,83)   3 T, 3 units of 15 Less, audio, OSCD-PE
           Volleyball
           Intra-individual variability

(R&R,81)   4 T (M, W), JHS, 6 Obs, live, T observation Schedule
           and Pupil observation Schedule
           Multiple discriminant analysis between: T contrast,
           days by T contrast, Cl contrast, days by Cl contrast.

(Ste,77)   12 T (elem, second), 3 observation/Cl, live, ORRPETB
           Grade level, gender, environment, teaching experience,
           T preparation.

(V,T,A,81) 20 Cl
           Indoor activities
           Process-Process (T behaviors - S behaviors)

(Yok,81)   101 Cl, JHS, SHS, Bales IA process analysis,
           video
           Volleyball
           School level, gender

Using the Anderson system to code 40 classes from the Video
Data Bank Project provide us with a view of the teaching act, of
how time is spent during a class. The comparison according to
grade level underscored very little difference in teacher's behavior profile (figure 2.1). Marked differences between master
teachers and student teachers were evidenced by Piéron, 1982
(figure 2.2). Feedback and silent observation differed strikingly.

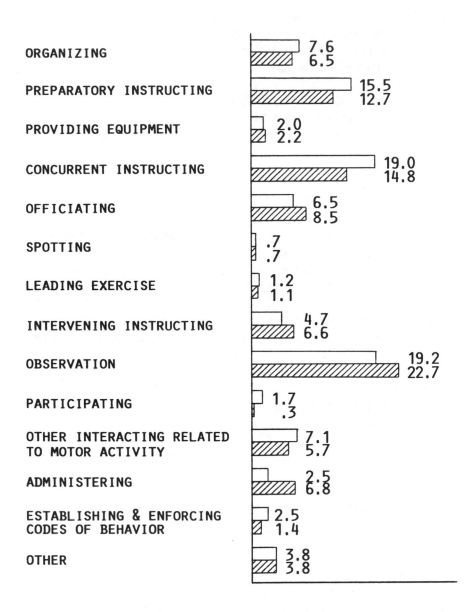

Figure 2.1 - Elementary and secondary comparisons of class time devoted to interactive function categories (Anderson & Barrette, 1978).

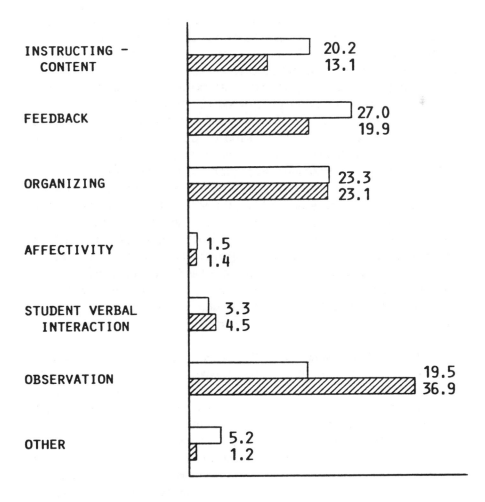

Figure 2.2 - Comparison of teacher's intervention time in high school classes. Master teachers ⬜ - Student teachers ▨

PRESENTATION OF CONTENT AND OF ACTIVITIES.

Content is the vehicle by which objectives are reached. It becomes the basis for determining the instructional materials to be used, the activities in which pupils will engage, and the procedures the teacher will employ. Good content is essential to good planning and good teaching.

Research has gathered very little data on how specific content information is presented to pupils. In most observational systems an alternative is usually envisaged for the teacher: (1) providing or giving the information; (2) seeking the information or helping the pupil to seek the information by a guided discovery approach or problem solving process. Many observation systems include categories labeled lecture and questioning, or structuring and solliciting. This kind of dichotomy seems to be of little help for supervision and counselling purposes. Systems which use post-script and subscript categories to further describe the nature of content (the Bake system of Batchelder & Keane (1983), for instance) have tended to alleviate the content problem to a large degree. However, the use of further subcategorisation detracts from the overall feasibility of natural recording and tends to be more helpful when categorising through a single channel alone. Perhaps successful content coding will have to await more sophisticated audio visual instrumentation and the appearance of saturation coding where many people are observing the same lesson on content from different perspectives.

QUANTITATIVE IMPORTANCE. The presentation of content amounts generally to 15 to 25 % of the events and of the interaction between the teacher and the students. This proportion varies considerably from one teacher to an another. In the Video Data Bank Project, Anderson & Barrette (1978b) observed an average of 14.2 % of the teachers time for the category "Preparatory instruction" i.e. providing information about the activity to be performed (rules, skills, ...), ranging from 1.1 to 38.4 % according to the teachers observed. The category "lecture" used by Freedman (1978) represented 14.8 % of the teachers behaviors in experienced teachers and only 5.4 % in student teachers. Piéron (1982a) found the same tendency to talk more in teachers than in student teachers.

As a rule, teachers did not spend long periods of time performing uninterrupted functions, but rather continuously shifted from one behavior to another seemingly attempting to keep up with the needs of the students and demands of the learning environment in a reactive or reflexive sense (Anderson & Barrette, 1978b).

Knowledge about the instructional model designed to help the student better perceive the information provided is important. An important aspect of the information concerning task presentation dealt with the use of a model (demonstration, charts, graphs ...) and sought to help the student perceive and catch the message. Anderson & Barrette (1978b) observed that teachers from their study used demonstration methods, an average of six times per lesson. On the other hand, Piéron (1982a) observed that in master teachers, approximately 50 % of the instruction was accompanied by different types of models (figure 2.3). Master teachers used a demonstration in 20 % of their instruction time, a pupils'demonstration in 18.3 %, a more sophisticated audiovisual aid in 13.9 % of this instructional time. They used also some movement simulation. Beginning teachers used a model less frequently than the master teachers. In beginners, a less accurate model like simulation was more frequent (Piéron, 1982a).

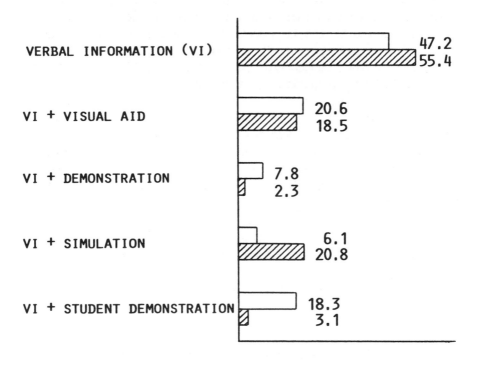

Figure 2.3 - Presentation of content by teachers in high school classes. Master teachers ☐ - Student teachers ▨

Considering a complete teaching unit (fifteen volleyball classes), Rink (1983) observed that a model was more frequently used in the beginning of the unit. It depended largely upon the introduction of a new technique, or of a new subject matter (Rink, 1983).

QUESTIONNING THE STUDENT. In classroom teaching, it has frequently been advocated that the use of questioning, especially those designed to tease out cognitive levels, was a preferred behavior. The principle evoked was that students remembered more information if they discovered it by themselves or were helped by a process of guided discovery from enlightened teachers. However, research data do not substantiate this principle. Rosenshine (1978) and Stalling & Kaskowitz (1974) summed up some of the results: more information is retained if the teacher asks mostly recall question during class, the frequency of academically focused direct questions at the two lower levels of the Bloom Taxonomy resulted in increased acquisition of basic arithmetic and reading skills, the frequency of factual, single-answer questions were correlated positively and significantly with achievement, whereas the frequency of more complex, difficult, or divergent questions had negative correlations.

In physical education, it has been reported in several studies that teachers asked fewer questions regarding the cognitive content of activities although questionning itself amounted to approximately 5 % of the all teaching behaviors observed in in-service teachers and in student teachers during the apprentice process (Freedman, 1978).

MULTIDIMENSIONAL STUDY OF SUBJECT MATTER PRESENTATION.

There are only a few studies specifically devoted to the presentation of content studied from the perspective of a multi-dimensional approach.

Levison (1978) devised an instrument to clarify the frequency with which the teacher focused the learner's attention on the environment. The observation system describes whether or not spatial, temporal or spatial/temporal components of the task environment are indicated; the variety of stimuli characteristics within the task environment; the simultaneous verbalization of a statement of motor plan with a statement about environmental stimuli.

In Catelli's study (1979), the categories were derived from concepts selected from the fields of educational philosophy, motor learning and the study of teaching. The dimensions provided information on the way the content was transmitted, by either providing for it or helping the student to seek it. Categories account for: directing students motor performance, describing it, evaluating, explaining, justifying, giving conditional directives, making inferences, defining - interpreting. These categories are related to outcomes, techniques & strategies and to environmental factors (conditions, situations, events, objects, position of objects). They are related to sport, game or contest rules and procedures. They concern the student motor performances, acts and decisions.

These studies were unfortunately limited to the study of validity and reliability. They were not systematically applied to provide descriptive data.

Box 2.4 - TEACHER SPECIFIC BEHAVIORS: INSTRUCTION: instruments of observation and methods of gathering data.

INSTRUMENTS:

(Bru,75)   Less introduction, 3 Obs, 10 audio
            Content validity, construct validity, reliability

(Cat,79   Catelli Category System (verbal and non verbal moves)
            Several stages involving 3 Obs, video (52 min)
            Inter-Observer reliability

(Lev,78)   Task environment
            3 Obs, video
            Inter- and intra-Observer reliability

(Rin,79)   Observation System for Content Development Physical
           Education (OSCD-PE)
           12 tapes, 4 Obs, elem, second, univ, video and live
           Dimensions: informing, refining, extending, applying
           Moderate to high reliability

TEACHER SPECIFIC BEHAVIOR: FEEDBACK: Instruments of observation
and methods of gathering data

INSTRUMENTS:

(Fis,74)   Fishman System
           Dimensions: form, direction, time, T intent, general
           referent, specific referent
           Validity (experts) & Reliability

(Har,74)   8 T (5 F & 3 M), 2 Obs
           Moderate to high reliability
           Dimensions: intent, content, form

FIELD STUDIES:

(Are,79)   30 T, 60 Cl, Feedback Cycle Descriptive System
           Tennis, swimming
           Gender, subject matter, environment (urban, rural),
           T preparation, age

(Arm,77)   40 T, 40 ST, video
(A&H,79)   Error detection proficiency
           Teaching experience

(B&C,82)   2 T (W), univ, 12x5 min observation, Fishman & Tobey
           Modern dance
           Descriptive

(Col,79)   3 T, 5 Less/T, T augmented feedback
           Golf
           Perception of feedback by experts, by T, by S

(P&D,80)   18 Cl., 1 MT (9 Cl), video
             FEED/ULg
             gymnastics, volley ball
             descriptive, T experience

(Pie,82a)   22 Cl, 12 MT, 10 ST, video
(P&D,82)   Gymnastics, volley
             T experience, school level

(P&D,82)   12 Cl, 12 MT, video
             Gymnastics, volley
             Process-process

(Qua,78)   24 T, elem, reactions of T
             Various subject matters
             Age, gender, size of Cl, grade levels, teaching
             styles, subject matters, Ts'rating of S Cl behavior

(Tob,77)   81 Cl, elem, second, video, Fishman system
(F&T,78)   Various subject matter
             Grade level, Cl size, T experience, subject matter,
             Process-process

MISCELLANEOUS:

(Car,80)   189 T, 2586 S, Critical Incidents
             Enthusiasm
             Comparison according to gender, to role (T vs S), to
             subject matter (English vs PE)

FEEDBACK.

In learning motor skills, sometimes individuals gain information about their responses without external help. It is feedback inherent in the task itself or intrinsic feedback. Informative or augmented feedback is information given to a learner to
help him/her repeat correct behaviors, eliminate incorrect behaviors, and achieve the desired outcomes. The need for informative
feedback to improve and sustain performance is an essential
learning experience. Instructional theorists traditionally have

viewed teacher feedback following a learner's response as a critical pedagogical operation.

Feedback is considered to be located at a crossroads of the learning and teaching processes. In teaching, informative feedback exceeds a mere knowledge of results or information gained about the correctness or incorrectness of ones'behaviors. Feedback is included in learning models for skill acquisition (Gentile, 1972; Singer & Dick, 1974) as well as in models for teaching effectiveness (Bloom, 1979; Carroll, 1963).

MODEL OF STUDY. Feedback is seen as the result of a series of questions asked and of decisions made by the teacher. The quality of feedback relies heavily on several teaching skills and decision making abilities. The model of "Clinical Diagnosis as a Pedagogical Skill" described by Hoffman (1983) is of great help in organizing the knowledge in the domain (figure 2.4).

The following of teaching skills, decisions and questions helps to arrange research data in this area of teacher intervention:

(1) Observation of the performance and identification of errors;

(2) The decision to be made about reacting or not reacting to the motor skill performance;

(3) Type of feedback. When deciding to react, the teacher must choose between a reaction giving information or an intervention simply reinforcing the student's behavior.

(4) In informative feedback the kind of information is important. Answering this question represents the focus of multidimensional analyses in feedback.

(5) How does the student respond to the teacher's feedback?

(6) Does the teacher follow through with the feedback and observe student's new trials?

The two last points deal with the post feedback behaviors.

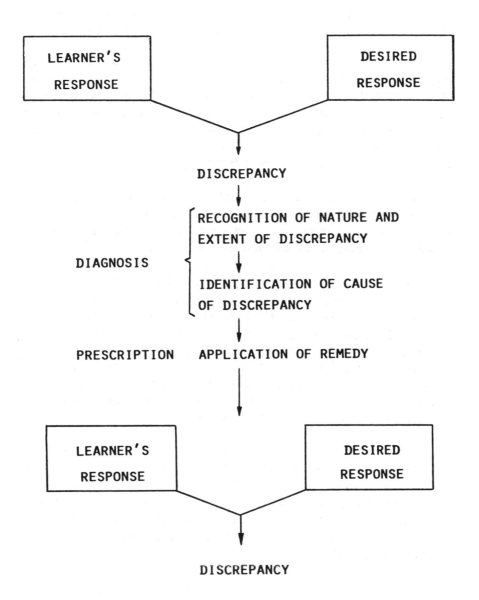

Figure 2.4 – Diagnostic prescriptive model of skills
teaching (Hoffman, 1983).

OBSERVATION OF STUDENT'S PERFORMANCE. There seems to be general agreement in models and paradigms of the teaching process that observation of pupil learning behaviors should be an important skill for teachers. The content of the feedback message depends largely on the instructor's ability to analyze the skill, to determine those factors critical to proficiency at a particular stage of learning, to identify the aspects of the response which are preventing the learner from attaining the skill objectives and provide feedback relative to these factors (Barrett, 1979a, 1979b, 1983; Craft, 1977; Hoffman, 1983).

Observation is a special skill; it involves more than just watching what is going on. Alertness, sensitivity, and ability to identify and to assess crucial behavior and relationships. A key to useful observation is knowing what should be seen.

As stated above, the content of the feedback depends largely on the teachers'ability to identify errors. Armstrong (1977), Armstrong and Hoffman (1979) compared the detection error proficiency of experienced tennis teachers and inexperienced tennis students teachers. Experienced teachers were significantly more accurate in detecting errors than the novice teachers. The differences appeared to be mainly due to fewer false alarms expressed by experienced teachers. Novice teachers reported the presence of an error when the error was not demonstrated.

DECISION MAKING. After having identified an error the teacher has to decide whether a reaction is necessary or not. When deciding to react, the teacher is confronted with another question: Does the student need more practice or additional information concerning his/her performance? If the learner needs more practice, the teacher can react by praising, encouraging or by positive evaluation.

We do not know any specific observation study dealing with the process of making this decision, the teacher's way of thinking to decide what to say to the student about personal performance.

Most of the process studies related to augmented feedback can be distributed in two broad categories dealing with: (1) the quantitative part of feedback in the total teacher pupil relationship; (2) a more qualitative information related to the complex structure of feedback studied through multidimensional analyses.

QUANTITATIVE IMPORTANCE OF FEEDBACK IN THE TEACHING RELATIONSHIP.

One or several feedback categories are included in many teacher or coach behavior category systems (Demarteau & Piéron, 1978; Freedman, 1978; Piéron, 1982a; Stewart, 1977), or in coach observation schedules (Brunelle et al, 1978a; Smith, Smoll & Hunt, 1977; Tharp & Gallimore, 1976).

Feedback occurrence was shown to be largely variable. It ranged from less than 10 % to more than 25 % of the behaviors recorded and from less than one feedback to approximately four per minute. Piéron (1982a) reported that feedback represented 27.0 % of the interactions in master teachers and 19.9 % in student teachers. The proportion of feedback seems to be much lower in several other studies. Positive and negative feedback totalled 4.9 % in elementary school teachers, 6.33 % in junior high school teachers and 3.27 % in senior high school teachers (Stewart, 1977). This amount must be augmented with corrective feedback recorded in the study. They cannot be clearly estimated by levels, but they ranged from 0.7 to 16.1 % according to teachers (Stewart, 1977). The part of feedback in teachers intervention was observed to amount to 9.0 % in in-service teachers and to 9.21 % in student teachers (Freedman, 1978). It must be reminded that percentages are hard to compare. The most secure means to compare the quantitative importance of feedback is surely the intervention rate or the frequency of occurrence.

Besides these descriptive data, comparisons concerned the influence of teacher preparation (Stewart, 1977), the influence of teaching experience (Freedman, 1978; Stewart, 1977), the influence of grade levels (Piéron & Delmelle, 1981), the influence of subject matter taught (Piéron, 1982a).

Fishman & Tobey (1978) observed an intervention rate close to one per minute. They have observed 81 classes from the Video Data Bank Project (Anderson, 1975). The interindividual variability in issuing feedback was extremely high. The number of feedback issued per lesson ranged from 1 to 297, with a median of 47. In another study, Arena (1979) observed 30 swimming and tennis teachers. The average occurence of feedback was equal to 1.17 per minute. These findings were confirmed by Brunelle et al. (1983) on primary and secondary school students. They used an adaptation of the Coaching Behavior Assessment System (CBAS) to observe the teachers. Several behavior modification studies from Ohio State University reported an intervention rate averaging around one occurrence per minute.

The intervention rate of master teachers observed in several studies completed at the University of Liège was largely higher than in the previously reported studies (Piéron & Delmelle, 1981; Piéron & V. Delmelle, 1983). These teachers put a stronger emphasis on content in their teaching. The lesson rate of feedback averaged at four per minute, ranging from 2.1 to 8.3 (Piéron & Delmelle, 1981). Brunelle & de Carufel (1982) reported figures as high as 5.5 feedback per minute in two selected dance teachers, figures confirmed by Piéron & V. Delmelle (1983).

Master teachers were observed to emit significantly more frequent feedback than student teachers (Piéron & Delmelle, 1981).

The intervention rate showed a trend to increase from junior high school level to senior high school level (Piéron & Delmelle, 1981). Brunelle et al. (1983) observed a lower rate at the elementary school level than at the secondary level.

Findings were also contradictory when subject matter taught were compared. Fishman & Tobey (1978) observed more frequent feedback occurrences in dual sports that in team sport. Intervention rate was higher in volleyball than in gymnastics, although information conveyed in teacher's feedback was equally distributed in both subject matters (Piéron & R. Delmelle, 1983).

We are still far from a clear image of how frequent feedback occurs according to context and programme variables.

After identification a performance error, teachers must first decide if a reaction is necessary or not. When deciding to react, the teacher must assess whether the student more urgent

Table 2.2 - Feedback intervention rates.

Rate 1 Fb every N sec.	Teachers	Authors
UNDETERMINED SUBJECT MATTER		
45	Teachers	Fishman & Tobey (1978)
30	Teachers	Brunelle et al. (1980)
40	Teachers	Brunelle et al. (1983)
GYMNASTICS		
11	Master Teachers	Piéron & Devillers (1980)
18	Student-Teachers	
16	Master Teachers	Piéron & R. Delmelle (1983)
20	Teachers	Piéron, Neto, Carreiro da Costa (1985)
VOLLEYBALL		
14	Master Teachers	Piéron & R. Delmelle (1983)
BASKETBALL		
29	Teachers	Piéron, Neto & Carreiro da Costa (1985)
DANCE		
15	Master Teachers	Piéron & V. Delmelle (1983)
22	Beginning Teachers	
11	Teachers	Brunelle & de Carufel (1982)
TENNIS AND SWIMMING		
51	Teachers	Arena (1979)

need is information or additional practice trials. In the latter case, reinforcement, encouragement or approbatory statements can be sufficient.

If additional information seems to be necessary to improve the performance, then a feedback is issued.

SIMPLE EVALUATION OR SPECIFIC FEEDBACK.

"Stallings & Kaskowitz (1974) correlated different types of feedback with learning outcomes. Their results suggested that the topic of feedback (academic, behavioral, other tasks) is more important than type of feedback (positive, negative, neutral). When the topic of feedback was academic, i.e. reading and mathematics, 19 out of the 20 correlations were positive and 13 of them significant, and this held whether the type of feedback was positive or negative. When the feedback related to other tasks (music, art, dance, science), the correlation was always negative with regard to the outcome measures, regarless of type of feedback." (Bennett, 1978).

"The type of feedback that teachers provide to students also seemed to be important. Feedback that was academic in nature correlated positively with achievement." (Berliner, 1979).

In several studies, large differences were observed in the structure of augmented feedback. From 25 to 50 % of feedback took an evaluative aspect by which teachers informed learners about their performance in using a positive or negative sentence. Teachers frequently avoided providing them with specific information related to the performance. It seems that some teachers intended only to rate the performance rather than to seek motor behavior modifications through reinforcement techniques (Fishman & Tobey, 1978; Piéron, 1982a).

As a rule, it must be noticed that ratios between simple unspecific feedback and specific feedback diverge according to their approbatory or disapproving character. Usually teachers expresses a whole satisfaction. Their dissatisfaction is completed by additional statements describing the error, explaining the movement to perform or prescribing some movement modifications (Brunelle et al., 1976; Piéron, 1982a). It could be thought that such a behavior exerts an attenuating effect on the disapproving statement.

APPROVING FEEDBACK, DISAPPROVING FEEDBACK, SPECIFIC FEEDBACK. Frequently, teaching analysis schedules discriminate between positive, negative or neutral aspects of feedback (Brunelle et al., 1978b; Brunelle et al., 1983; Freedman, 1978; Hughley, 1973; Morgenegg, 1978; Quarterman, 1978; Piéron & Hacourt, 1979; Rife, 1973; Stewart, 1977). This distinction corresponds to the idea of class climate or relies on a principle from operant psychology concerning the expected long term beneficial effect of reinforcement.

Frequent approbatory statements are supposed to help create a supportive climate in the class. A climate resulting from dominantly disapproving statements is supposed to create less favorable learning conditions. Caution must be taken in associating automatically approbatory with positive and disapproving with negative. Some disapproving statements can be considered a challenge students to improve performance by students.

The findings provided by different studies lead to a clouded image. A marked difference was observed when comparing the positive and the negative aspects of feedback studied in the Video Data Bank Project and in studies made at the University of Liège. The negative aspect of the reaction (56.1 %) was more frequent than the positive aspect (42.1 %) in the first study. Observing the same tapes, Morgenegg (1978) reported 38.8 % of positive feedback, 19.4 % negative and 29.4 % neutral feedback. Piéron and collaborators observed frequently a ratio approximating 3 to 1 in favour of positive or approbative interventions. Freedman (1978) observed that occurrences of positive feedback were more variable than negative forms.

MULTIDIMENSIONAL ANALYSIS OF FEEDBACK.

Multidimensional observation systems were devised in considering feedback as a central element of the analysis. These studies aimed at describing mostly form, content, intent, general and specific referents, direction of feedback, and time of delivery (Table 2.3)

Table 2.3 - Dimensions and categories of feedback.

FORM
      Auditory
      Auditory - Tactile
      Auditory - Visual

DIRECTION
      Individual
      Group
      Class

INTENT
      Evaluation
      Description
      Prescription
      Comparison

CUE RELEVANCY
      Cue relevant
      Cue irrelevant

TIME
      Condurrent
      Terminal
      Delayed

GENERAL REFERENT
      Whole Movement
      Part of Movement
      Outcome of Movement

SPECIFIC REFERENT
      Force
      Space
      Rate

There are a few descriptive studies of teacher's feedback. Like in other fields of the study of the teaching relationship, they vary consistently according to observed classes, and to context and programme variables.

Tobey (1977), Fishman & Tobey (1978) used 81 out the 83 lessons videotaped in the Teachers College Video Data Bank Project. Though a rigourous sampling concerning school location, school level, environmental variables, biass exist when considering subject matter taught, it is hard to discriminate between subject matter and teaching objectives. Nevertheless that is probably the most comprehensive study in that field of observation. In the whole study reported in Tobey's doctorate these (1977) comparisons were made according to school level (elementary or secondary), class size (0-20, 21-40, over 41 pupils), students gender (boys, girls, coed classes), years of teaching experience (0-5, 6-10, over 11), subject matter (dual sports, team sports, team sports, games and others), practice or competition. There were so many possible comparisons that no real discussion of the differences found was attempted.

Several other studies (Table 2.4) deal with a lower number of classes but differentiate more on the subject matter taught: gymnastics and volley-ball (Piéron & R. Delmelle, 1981, 1982, 1983), swimming and tennis (Arena, 1979), dance (Brunelle & de Carufel, 1982; Piéron & V. Delmelle, 1983).

Observations deal with student teachers (Piéron, 1982a) to master teachers (Brunelle & de Carufel, 1982; Piéron & Delmelle, 1981).

Each study has its own originality. It will be underscored when useful.

FORM OF THE FEEDBACK (figure 2.5). There are very few divergences in categories used in the analysis of the form of feedback. Common points in coding this dimension of feedback make comparison of data provided by different studies relatively easy. Feedback can be verbal (perceived through audition), kinesthetic (or tactile) or visual. The verbal feedback can be supplemented by visual or/and kinesthetic information.

Table 2.4 - Comparison of feedback in gymnastics and in volleyball (Piéron & Delmelle, 1981)

	GYMNASTICS		VOLLEYBALL	
	Mean	Min.-Max.	Mean	Min.-Max.
Intent				
Evaluation	34.7	16.1-47.8	27.3	22.0-33.6
Description	24.3	16.5-29.9	25.7	17.4-34.2
Prescription	28.9	19.8-43.1	41.2	31.7-46.5
Affectivity	5.5	1.6-17.7	4.3	1.5-11.1
Questioning	7.5	0.0-18.1	1.5	0.3- 3.7
Content				
No content	39.6	23.4-56.3	28.3	21.4-39.1
Cognitive	52.9	35.7-65.8	63.6	49.3-72.3
Perceptive	7.5	1.1-14.6	8.0	1.5-17.4
Form				
Auditive	85.5	72.4-92.2	83.9	71.2-92.8
Tactile	1.4	0.0- 4.8	0.3	0.0- 0.7
Visual	0.7	0.0- 1.8	1.4	0.0- 4.3
Mixed, kinesthetic	6.3	1.1-12.7	2.8	0.0- 9.8
Mixed, visual	6.2	2.7- 9.5	11.6	3.3-18.6
Direction				
Class	16.4	9.1-29.1	13.3	5.6-30.7
Group	7.0	1.0-13.9	12.5	2.8-28.3
Student	76.6	62.5-89.9	74.2	61.9-91.1

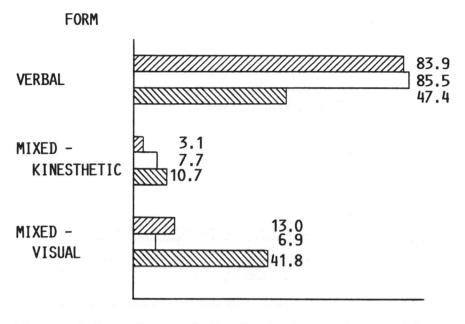

Figure 2.5 - Form of feedback in various subject matters.
Volleyball ▨ Gymnastics ☐ Dance ▨

    Augmented feedback was observed to be predominantly verbal. From 70 to 95 % of feedback occurrences were classified in this category in studies reviewed (Arena, 1979; Fishman & Tobey, 1978; Harrington, 1974; Piéron & Devillers, 1980; Piéron & Delmelle, 1982). Piéron & Delmelle (1982) observed that 84 % of the feedback emitted was purely verbal, the interindividual variability ranged from 71.2 to 92.8 %. This part of auditory or verbal feedback in the total feedback was slightly higher at the senior high school level than at the junior high school level. Teachers more frequently provided different kinds of models to supplement their verbal information with younger pupils. This aspect of informative feedback seemed to very little with student gender, subject matter taught or gender of teachers.

    DIRECTION OF FEEDBACK (figure 2.6). Like the form of feedback, the direction can be distributed in well differentiated categories presenting few difficulties for coding by observers. Feedback was usually directed towards the whole class, a group or a single student.

DIRECTION

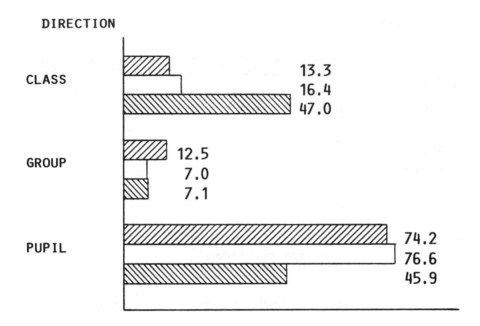

Figure 2.6 - Direction of feedback in various subject matters.
Volleyball ▨▨▨   Gymnastics ▭   Dance ▨▨▨

   In most studies, feedback was directed towards single students in approximately 75 % of the observations (Arena, 1979;
Fishman & Tobey, 1978; Piéron & Devillers, 1980; Piéron &
Delmelle, 1981). Some divergences occurred according to whether
the second main direction is towards a group or towards the
entire class. Teachers observed in the studies made at the University of Liege showed a tendency to provide more feedback
towards the class (15 %) than towards a group (less than 10 %)
except in team sports settings. Arena (1979) observed the same
tendency with more frequent feedback directed to the class than
to the group. However, the overwhelming part of feedback was
directed towards single students, more than 90 %. Fishman & Tobey
(1978) observed the opposite tendency.

   It is logical that a larger part of feedback would be directed towards groups in team sports classes (Piéron & Delmelle,
1982).

Two studies gathered similar data but largely departed from the above description. In dance classes, the usual organization implies a feedback predominantly oriented towards the whole class. Approximately 50 % of feedback pertained to this category (Brunelle & de Carufel, 1982; Piéron & V. Delmelle, 1983).

INTENT OF FEEDBACK (figure 2.7). The intent of feedback is probably one of the most important dimensions to be studied in

INTENT

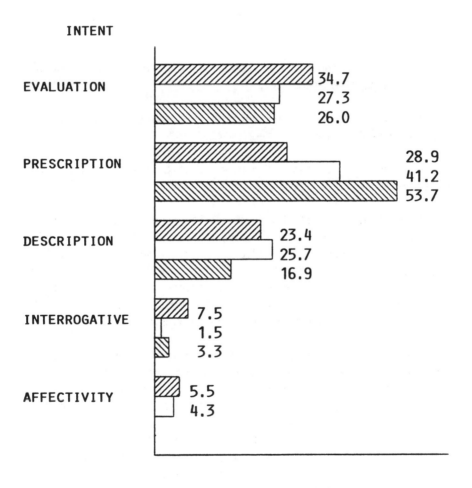

Figure 2.7 - Intent of feedback in various subject matters.
Volleyball ▨   Gymnastics ☐   Dance ▧

the multidimensional approach of informative feedback. Definitions given by Fishman & Tobey (1978) can illustrate this dimension of studying augmented feedback. It intends to provide:

(1) an appraisal of the performance of a motor skill (evaluative feedback);

(2) an account of the performance of a motor skill (descriptive feedback);

(3) an analogy to the performance of a motor skill (comparative feedback);

(4) instruction for the subsequent performance of a motor skill (prescriptive feedback);

(5) an attudinal or motivational set toward the performance of a motor skill (affective feedback).

Feedback can be part of a process of guided discovery and therefore be interrogative.

More than half of the feedback issued were categorized as "evaluative feedback" (53 %). Data provided by Arena (1979) confirmed this observation: 48.0 of feedback was affective, i.e. intending to provide an appraisal of the skill, or to provide motivation. Corrective feedback, intending to provide instructions for the future performance of the motor skill amounted to 42.2 %. Descriptive feedback amounted to 9.8 %.

The part of evaluative feedback observed in several studies made at the University of Liège by Piéron and collaborators was markedly lower. Evaluative feedback rarely exceeded 35 % of all feedback provided. This dimension was predominant in gymnastics and at the junior high school level. Prescription happened to be a frequent intent of feedback at the secondary school level. Descriptive intent amounted to more than 20 % of feedback provided. Interrogative feedback occurred less frequently averaging around 5 % of all feedback issued.

REFERENT OF FEEDBACK. In assisting the pupil in organizing what alternative strategies, he may use in preparing his next response the teacher can provide feedback of two types: (1) information concerning the movement's execution, and (2) information about the degree of goal attainment.

Feedback was observed to be frequently concerned with the whole movement (provided about multiple components in the performance of a motor skill) than to specific components of the performance or even to the outcome or the movement goal (Fishman & Tobey, 1978).

When focusing on the specific referent of feedback, it was observed that the intervention emphasized mostly the direction, level magnitude of the movement (space), rather than time or duration (rate) or strength and power (force) expended in the performance of the motor skill. Teachers observed by Fishman & Tobey (1978) directed 85 % of their feedback with an emphasis on the spatial components of the task.

Augmented feedback was almost equally distributed between a focus on knowledge of results (52.9 %) and knowledge of performance (47.1 %) (Arena, 1979).

CUE RELEVANCY. One important dimension of feedback was developed by Arena (1979) and dealt with the relationship between instructional cues and augmented feedback provided by the teacher during the motor skill acquisition. Feedback was categorized according to the fact that it provided information about the response just performed and related to a cue given during prior instruction, or not related to prior instruction. Augmented feedback coded in the Arena's study showed that 46.8 % of initial feedback was not cue relevant. This percentage dropped to 26.9 % when teachers followed up on their initial feedback by another feedback. Such a level of irrelevancy is disquieting for the quality of teaching and the need for a good presentation of subject matter is underlined.

POST FEEDBACK BEHAVIORS (figure 2.8). Post feedback student and teacher behaviors play an important role when pursuing learning objectives. Two aspects must be considered: How is the student responding? How is the teacher behaving after the first feedback? The "How the student is responding" dimension of feedback analysis must occasion extreme caution. Resistance to

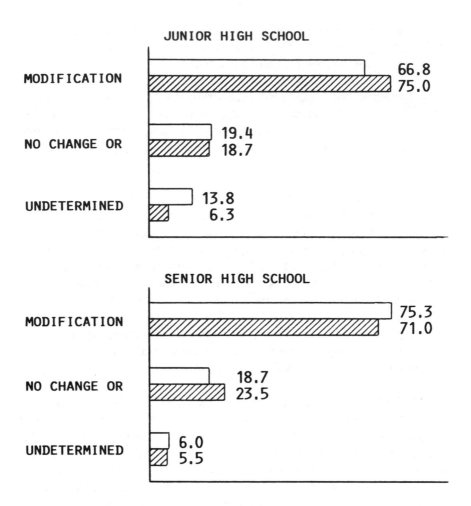

Figure 2.8 - Postfeedback behaviors.
Descriptive feedback
Prescriptive feedback

attributing a causality relationship when a teacher's feedback is accompagnied by some student expected change in motor performance must occur. When an evaluative feedback is given, no clear information is provided to students to help them rethink their motor plan for the next performance. When informative feedback is provided the student receiving the feedback can be identified and observed until performing again on the same task. The observer has to evaluate if the new performance is corrected or no change occurred or whether or not the performance is deteriorating. Only short term decisions can be made. The process is time consuming and reliability is observed to be lower than with other dimensions of the observational system (Piéron & Delmelle, 1982). Feedback provided by master teachers was more frequently accompanied by an expected student response than with feedback provided by student teachers. Important differences were observed when comparing the intent of feedback. Descriptive feedback seems to be more effective at the senior high school level than at the junior high school level. On the other hand, prescriptive feedback was more frequently accompanied by an expected change in junior high school student (Piéron & Delmelle, 1982).

In her study, Arena (1979) observed the cycles of initial feedback plus follow-up augmented feedback. 31.1 % of a total of 1,454 initial feedback was followed by additional augmented responses of the teachers (see table 2.7). It was also observed that several initial feedback was followed by up to 8 additional informative feedbacks.

Table 2.5 - The augmented feedback cycles (adapted from Arena, 1979).

	N (1454)	%
No follow-up	1008	69.3
1 cycle (initial feedback plus 1 follow-up)	313	21.5
2 cycles (initial feedback plus 2 follow-up)	60	4.1
3 cycles (initial feedback plus 3 follow-up)	48	3.3
4 cycles (initial feedback plus 4 follow-up)	4	0.3
5 cycles (initial feedback plus 5 follow-up)	9	0.6
6 cycles (initial feedback plus 6 follow-up)	8	0.6
7 cycles (initial feedback plus 7 follow-up)	2	0.1
8 cycles (initial feedback plus 8 follow-up)	2	0.1

AFFECTIVE BEHAVIORS.

Theorists in physical education grand special attention to affective behaviors in the management of a class. The application of the reinforcement theory to physical education was largely developped by Rushall & Siedentop (1972). Affective behaviors are systematically recorded in almost all observation systems dealing with the overall image of teachers'behaviors. In systems adapted from Flanders System of Interaction Analysis categories are used to record praise and encouragement, and to record events of authority. No verbal cues such as smiles, nods with smile, applauses, pats on shoulders are categorized in CAFIAS.

Other systems like those used at the Ohio State University by Stewart (1977), Freedman (1978) and by Quarterman (1978) discriminate between positive and negative behaviors. These authors put some positive valence on interventions like hustling (teacher using verbal statements or gesture to activate or intensify efforts or previously instructed behaviors). It must be made clear that when viewing teaching behavior, it is important not to evaluate behavior as positive or negative independent of its effects upon students. For example, the teacher we see as hypercritical may be seen by his students as a person who sets high standards because he cares about them.

Reference is made to general praise when the intervention does not concern a skill attempt. The category "hustle" seems to come from the coaching behaviors where such kind of effort intensification is frequent (Tharp & Gallimore, 1976). Other events receive a negative valence such as "nags" when the teacher scolds a student for an undesirable behavior. When this scolding is done with high intensity, it is categorized as "nasties". It happens that a special category is devoted to punishment.

Nevertheless the quantitative importance of these behaviors is very often considerably limited furing physical education lessons. In spite of their low rate of occurrence, they seem to play a prominent role in establishing the climate of the class and they exert probably a striking role in the teaching process.

Research in the classroom did not showed a clear relationship between a positive climate and student achievement, although it is fairly widely confirmed that a negative climate tends to exert a deterimental effect on students'motivation to improve.

Data from observation of physical education classes do not show a consistent image in the use of positive and negative interventions. They were approximately equally distributed in teachers observed by Freedman (1978): 2.71 % vs 3.48 % in in-service teachers, 3.33 % vs 3.43 % in student teachers. The tendency in the Stewart's observations was also unclear: more praise at the elementary level, equal use of both types of inter-ventions at the junior high school level and more praise and hustle at the senior high school level.

The research results show that there has been a decrease in teacher criticism in classes during the latter part of the 1970s and early part of the 1980s than there was prior to this time. The absence of the use of criticism may be interpreted as a strong sign of greater teacher emphasis upon constructive, affec-tive climate. The effect here, though, can also induce greater student decision-making which, in turn, has, in many cases, resulted in a negative climate. It appears than more research is needed into the patterns of teaching and student - teacher inter-action to tease out what kind of behaviors tend to follow criti-cism and under what circumstances. It is likely that the answer to this question will await developments in the process-product instrumentation of tomorrow.

ENTHUSIASM.

This concept is frequently linked to the idea of excellence in teaching. Enthusiastic behavior is looked at as a characteris-tic of good teachers.

Several questions arise immediately. How can enthusiasm be defined? How can it be measured? Is it a characteristic intima-tely linked to the personnality of the teacher or is it a tea-ching skill that can be learned, practiced and improved?

The measure of enthusiasm is dependent on its definition. Do we consider it a large concept observed or measured by high inferential systems or can it be reduced to fragmentary behaviors more easily observed.

From their review of literature, Locke & Woods (1982) concluded that it can be observed with acceptable reliability with high inference instruments.

In classroom teaching, Rosenshine & Furst (1973) conducted the most comprehensive survey of reputable research undertaken to their time. They factor-analysed the results presented in more than 200 credible research abstracts. Loading very highly, in fact, third of 11 variables, was the factor of teacher enthusiasm. We accept the inference of Locke & Woods (1982) that enthusiasm is not difficult to describe but reject the conclusion that its affect is difficult to measure. Such concrete behaviors as attendance, enjoyment, persistence and mutually initiating verbal and non-verbal behaviors are measurable. It has been consistent finding of CAFIAS's research that patterns of interaction which exhibit teacher enthusiasm have produced higher forms of student functioning and behavior. We do believe, however, that much more research is needed in this important area.

MANAGEMENT OF THE CLASS.

Functions of organization or management account frequently for more than 20 % of the total of verbal teaching events. A high level of managerial behavior seems to characterize the teaching of physical education. These interventions group statements dealing with providing equipment, discipline and the behavioral conduct of the class with the pace of exercises imposed by teacher and commands at the start and the end of an activity. The managerial behaviors reflect a praiseworthy concern to provide pupils with the best possible conditions of practice skill and to allow for repetition. They are prerequisite conditions to efficient learning. However these behaviors do not produce a direct educational effect on the learner.

Research on tasks and accountability has begun to provide us with some insight into the management of the class. Qualitative observation was used by Tousignant (1982) and by Alexander (1982).

Alexander (1982) observed that tasks were stated in both instructional and managerial systems. Managerial tasks were monitored closely by the teacher, showing little modification over time. Instructional tasks were less closely monitored.

SILENT OBSERVATION.

Silent observation of the student is reported to take quite a large part of teacher's time around 15-20 % (Anderson & Barrette, 1978b; Piéron, 1982a). Master teachers spent less time in this behavior than student teachers (Piéron, 1982a). There is no information yet provided which accurately accords a description of mental operations of teachers or of the process by which they decide to make an intervention. Some work in West Germany touches on this important factor but little concrete resolution is yet to hand.

CHAPTER 3

TEACHER-STUDENT INTERACTION

Climate of the class.
Flanders Interaction Analysis System (FIAS)
Cheffers Adaptation of Flanders Interaction Analysis System (CAFIAS)
Picture of teaching relationship through teacher - student inter-
 action analysis
Variations according to context variable
    Gender
    School or grade level
    Normal adapted or mainstreamed classes
Variations according to programme variables
    Decision making
    Teaching styles
Job satisfaction
The expectancy phenomenon in teacher - student interaction
Teaching patterns
    Observation instruments
    General interaction patterns
    Variations according to context: gender and school level
    Methodology

CLIMATE OF THE CLASS.

The expression "Climate of the Class" concerns concepts and data gathered mainly through the Flanders Interaction Analysis System (FIAS) or through Flanders adapted systems.

The first study of physical education teachers'behaviors focused on this aspect of the climate of the class. Bookhout (1966, 1967) observed nine woman teachers with a modified form of OScAR (Observation Schedule And Record) and identified by factor analysis six patterns of teacher's behavior among these physical education female teachers. Two were climate related: the integrative interaction pattern was positively related to the supportive climate; the restraining direction pattern was positively related to the defensive climate. Four other patterns were called activity direction, skill perfection, participation and aloofness. They were negligibly related to class climate. In Bookhout's study, the climate of the class was assessed by administering Reed's pupil inventory.

FLANDERS INTERACTION ANALYSIS SYSTEM (FIAS).

The source of inspiration of Flanders can be found in Anderson research (1939) on dominative and integrative behaviors and in Lewin, Lippitt and White research (1939) on the social climate of a class. It is not necessary to expand largely on this topic.

The findings of Anderson are based on the study of pre-school, primary and elementary school classrooms involving different teachers and extending over several years. According to Anderson, the behavior of the teacher, more than that of any individual, sets the climate of the class. The rule is that: domination incites further domination and integration stimulates further integration. It was also stressed that the pattern of a teacher developed in one year is likely to persist the following year with completely different pupils. When a teacher's integrative contacts increase, pupils show an increase in spontaneity and initiative, voluntary social contributions, and acts of problem solving.

Teacher-Student Interaction

The approach developed by Flanders (1970) relies on several
assumptions. The teacher would exert two types of influence on
the class, namely a dominant, authoritarian, direct influence
and/or integrative, democratic influence.

These two kinds of influence have been defined in terms of
verbal behaviors as follows:

"Direct influence consists of stating the teacher's own
opinion or ideas, directing the pupils' action, criticizing
his behavior, or justifying the teacher's authority or use
of that authority.

Indirect influence consists of soliciting the
opinions or ideas of the pupils, applying or enlarging on
those opinions or ideas, praising and encouraging the participation of pupils, or clarifying and accepting their feelings." (Flanders, 1970).

It must be strongly emphasized that refering to non direc-
tive theories, the indirect approach was frequently misinter-
preted as the only good way to teach and the direct approach a a
poor approach to teaching. It is important to keep in mind that
data gathered through interaction analysis systems should not
elicit value judgement such as good or bad. As stated by Cheffers
et al. (1981), value designations are properly the area of the
teacher's under study. If the descriptive data matches their
goals and objectives, then behaviors may be termed "appropriate".

Full respect must be paid to the Flanders contribution to
the study of physical education teaching. Many observation systems found their origin in the Flanders System. Many other studies include categories from the original Flanders Interaction
Analysis System. It can be considered as the starting point for a
host of studies describing the teaching of physical education and
studies using a presage - process approach.

Data gathered through the FIAS can be dealt with in several
ways:

* percentages and ratios: Student Talk (ST), Teacher Talk
(TT), ST/TT ratio, Indirect/Direct ratio;

Table 3.1 – Categories of Flanders Interaction Analysis System (Flanders, 1970).

TEACHER TALK

Indirect

1. ACCEPTS FEELING: Accepts and clarifies the feeling tone of the students in a non-threatening manner. Feelings may be positive or negative. Predicting or recording feelings included.

2. PRAISES OR ENCOURAGES: Praises or encourages student action or behavior, jokes that release tension, but not at the expense of another individual; nodding head or saying "um hum?" or "go on" are included.

3. ACCEPTS OR USES IDEAS OF STUDENTS: Clarifying, building, or developing ideas suggested by a student; as teacher brings more of his own ideas into play, shift to category 5.

4. ASKS QUESTIONS: Asking a question about content or procedure with the intent that a student answer.

Direct

5. LECTURING: Giving facts or opinions about content or procedures; expressing his own ideas, asking rhetorical questions.

6. GIVING DIRECTIONS: Directions, commands, or orders with which a student is expected to comply.

7. CRITICIZING OR JUSTIFYING AUTHORITY: Statements intended to change student behavior from non-acceptable to acceptable pattern; bawling someone out; stating why the teacher is doing what he is doing; extreme self-reference.

STUDENT TALK

8. STUDENT TALK-RESPONSE: Talk by students in response to teacher. Teacher initiates contact or solicits student statement.

9. STUDENT TALK-INITIATION: Talk by students which they initiate. If "calling on" student is only to indicate who may talk next, observer must decide whether student wanted to talk. If he did, use this category.

10. SILENCE OR CONFUSION: pauses, short periods of silence, and periods of confusion in which communication cannot be understood by the observer.

* areas in the interaction matrix (Figure 3.1);

Category	Classification		Category	1	2	3	4	5	6	7	8	9	10	Total
Accepts feelings	Teacher talk	Indirect influence	1	Area E										
Praise			2											
Student idea			3											
Asks questions		Direct influence	4	"Content cross"							Area I			
Lectures			5											
Gives directions			6						Area F					
Criticism			7											
Student response	Student talk		8	Area G				Area H			Area J			
Student initiation			9											
Silence			10											
			Total	Area A				Area B			Area C	D		
				Indirect teacher talk				Direct teacher talk			Student talk			

Figure 3.1 - Flanders Interaction Analysis System: matrix analysis

* percentages of the various categories;

* teaching patterns.

In the matrix analysis, the column totals indicated as areas "A", "B", "C" and "D" provide a general picture of the teacher-student interaction. They answer questions such as: "When someone was talking, what proportion of the time was used by students? By the teacher? Of the time that the teacher talked, what proportion of this talk involved indirect influence? Direct influence?

Content cross represents teacher behavior consisting primarily of teacher questions, lecture, and presentation of opinions, ideas, and information. Area E represents an emphasis in using extended indirect influence (accepting and enlarging upon student feelings, praising student behavior, and using student ideas).

Area F indicates the use of extended direct influence. Areas G, H, J, represent various student influences.

Teaching patterns are frequently derived from sequential observation system like FIAS and its adaptations.

The FIAS has been strongly criticized under several aspects and particularly its application in physical education. In classroom teaching, Dunkin & Biddle (1974) focused on the idea of commitment and on the weaknesses of non faceted systems.

Box 3.1 - Interaction Analysis: Studies & Papers Reviewed

Akkanen (1979)	(Akk79)
Allard (1979)	(All79)
Bahneman (1971)	(Bah71)
Batchelder (1975)	(Bat75)
Batchelder & Keane (1983)	*(B&K83)
Benjamin (1977)	(Ben77)
Bookhout (1966)	(Boo66)
Bookhout (1967)	(Boo67)
Brown (1980)	(Bro80)
Cheffers (1973)	(Che73)
Cheffers & Mancini (1978)	(C&M78)
Cheffers, Mancini, Martinek & Lydon (1980)	(Che80)
Cheffers (1983)	*(Che83)
Countiss (1976)	(Cou76)
Dobry & Svaton (1977)	(D&S77)
Dougherty (1970)	(Dou70)
Dougherty (1971)	*(Dou71)
Dougherty (1983)	*(Dou83)
Egger (1980)	*(Egg80)
Ewers (1981)	(Ewe81)
Gauthier (1980)	(Gau80)
Goldberger (1983)	*(Gol83)
Heinila (1979)	*(Hei79)
Heinila (1980)	(Hei80)

Heinila (1983)	(Hei83)
Imwold et al. (1984)	(Imw84)
Kasson (1974)	(Kas74)
Lewis (1974)	(Lew74)
Lewis K. (1979)	(Lew79)
Lombardo (1979)	(Lom79)
Lombardo (1982)	(Lom82)
Lombardo & Cheffers (1983)	(L&C83)
Lord (1981-82)	(Lor82)
Love & Roderick (1983)	*(L&R83)
Lucas (1978a)	(Luc78a)
Lunt (1974)	(Lun74)
Lydon (1978)	(Lyd78)
Mancini (1974)	(Man74)
Mancini & Cheffers (1983)	*(M&C83)
Mancini, Cheffers & Zaichkowsky (1976)	(M,C,Z,76)
Mancini, Wuest, Clark & Ridosh (1983)	(Man83)
Mancuso (1983)	*(Mso83)
Martinek (1976)	(Mar76)
Martinek & Karper (1984)	(M&K84)
Martinek & Mancini (1983)	*(M&M83)
Martinek, Zaichkowsky & Cheffers (1977)	(M,Z,C,77)
Mawsdley (1977)	(Maw77)
Mawson (1973)	(Maws73)
Melograno (1971)	(Mel71)
Melograno (1983)	*(Mel83)
Morgenegg (1978a)	(Mor78a)
Morgenegg (1978b)	(Mor78b)
Nygaard (1971)	(Nyg71)
Nygaard (1975)	(Nyg75)
Nygaard (1978)	(Nyg78)
Olson (1979)	(Ols79)
Olson (1982)	(Ols82)
Olson (1983a)	*(Ols83a)
Olson (1983b)	(Ols83b)
Piéron & Drion (1977a)	(P&D77a)
Piéron & Drion (1977b)	(P&D77b)
Piéron (1978)	(Pie78)
Rankin (1975)	(Ran75)
Rankin (1983)	*(Ran83)
Reponen (1979)	(Rep79)
Ritson, Smith & Twa (1982)	(R,S,T82)

Schempp (1982)   (Sch82)
Schempp, Cheffers & Zaichkowsky (1983) (S,C,Z83)
Splinter et al. (1979)   (Spl79)
Tavecchio et al. (1977)   (Tav77)
Taylor (1979)   (Tay79)
Timer (1983)   *(Tim83)
Twa (1979)   (Twa79)
Underwood (1978)   (Und78)
Underwood (1979)   *(Und79)
Underwood (1980)   (Und80)
Wuest & Coll (1982)   (Wue82)

* Papers dealing only with the description of instruments.

In physical education critics emphasized that the Flanders observational system was devised to record verbal behaviors in a subject matter privileging the non verbal behaviors. The original system was unable to take into account important teacher non verbal behaviors such as demonstration or affective behaviors like smiling, patting ... Feedback provided by the teacher, one of the most important function in teaching, is hardly accounted for the FIAS.

It was stressed that this system was off target when considering that specific objectives of physical education are of motor nature an that the behaviors recorded in the FIAS were only verbal in nature. The students motor behaviors must be categorized as "silence and confusion".

Another criticism is inherent to the sequential system of observation. As it is possible to record only one behavior at a time, priorities have to be maintained in such a way that teacher's behavior is frequently masking students' behaviors, and particularly their motor involvement. The system is ill suited to deal with a class organized and working by groups.

All these criticisms gave birth to many adaptations of the original system. Let us take some examples:

* Dougherty (1970, 1971) added one specific category to the original system : "meaningful non verbal activity" with an indication when the intervention was directed towards a single student;

* Piéron (1978b), Piéron & Drion (1977a, 1977b) used the observational system for the analysis of classroom interaction of Hough (1967). It took into account the feedback provided by the teacher, the demonstration, and a specific category for activity is limited by the sequential nature of the system.

* Mancuso (1972) developed several non verbal categories paralleling the verbal categories from the original Flanders system. The Mancuso study designed, tested and administered the observational instrument to enable to record and analyze both verbal and non verbal interaction in the secondary school physical education classroom. The instrument was designed by adapting existing instruments for the recording of verbal and non verbal interactions which had not been, however, designed for use in physical education. The investigator fused the Flanders' system of interaction analysis and the Love - Roderick non verbal categories into a single instrument and then added a purposeful motor activity category and a non-purposeful motor activity to the fused categories.

* In Europe, several authors devised adaptations by adding categories (Tavecchio et al., 1977), by adding dimensions to the original system (Heinila, 1979; Heinila, 1980), by subcategorizing (Hanke, 1979).

CHEFFERS ADAPTATION OF FLANDERS INTERACTION ANALYSIS SYSTEM (CAFIAS).

The most productive adaptation was developed in 1969 and published in 1973 by Cheffers. This author used also the idea of paralleling each category of the Flanders system with non verbal behaviors. They were considered as either encouraging or restricting communication between teacher and students. Non verbal communication was classified as facial expression and gestures, and postural positions. A conceptual change in the nature of preci-

Table 3.2 - The Categories of CAFIAS (2-17: Teacher Behaviors; 8-19: Student Behaviors; 10: Confusion; 20: Silence).

Cate-gories	RELEVANT BEHAVIORS	
	Verbal	Nonverbal
2-12	**2**	**12**
	A positive value assessment	**Face:** Smiles, nods energetically with smile, winks, laughs
	Praises, commends, jokes, encourages	**Posture:** Applauds by clapping hands or patting student on shoulder or head: shakes student' hand, embraces joyfully, laughs to encourage
3-13	**3**	**13**
	(No value implied)	(Elevates student performance onto a par with teacher performance)
	Accepts, clarifies, uses and develops suggestions and feelings of the student	**Face:** Nods without smiling, tilts head or sighs empathetically
	N.B. Flanders category one, which refers to teacher acceptance of student feelings and emotions, is included in this category. Coders are reminded to use 1 and 11 on the tally sheets. These behaviors are tallied separately for analysis purposes and included for parameter purposes in the matrix as 3s and 13s	**Posture:** Shakes hands, embraces sympathetically, places arm around shoulder or waist, catches an implement thrown by student, accepts facilitation from students, takes part in game with students, supports student during the activity or sports in gymnastics

Cate-gories	Verbal	Nonverbal
4–14	**4** Asks questions requiring student answers	**14** **Face:** Wrinkles brow, opens mouth, turns head with quizzical look **Posture:** Raises hands in air quizzically to expect answer, scratches head, cups hand to ear and stands still awaiting answer
5–15	**5** Gives facts, opinions, expresses ideas, or asks rhetorical questions	**15** **Face:** Whispers words audibly, sings or whistles **Posture:** Gesticulates, draws, writes, demonstrates activities, points, points to board
6–16	**6** Gives directions or orders that will result in immediate observable student response	**16** **Face:** Points with head, beckons with head, yells language other than recognizable words **Posture:** Points finger, blows whistle, holds body erect while barking commands, pushes a student in a given direction

Categories	Verbal	Nonverbal
7–17	**7**	**17**
	(A negative value assessment) Criticizes, expresses anger or distrust, uses sarcasm or extreme self-reference	**Face:** Grimaces, growls, frowns, drops head, throws head back in de derisive laughter rolls eyes, bites, spits, butts with head, shakes head
		Posture: Hits, pushes away, pinches, grapples with, pushes hands at student, drops hands in disgust, bangs table, damages equipment, throws things down
8–18	**8**	**18**
	Student response entirely predictable, such as obedience to orders and responses not requiring thinking beyond the comprehension phase or knowledge (after Bloom)	**Face:** Poker-face response, nods, shakes, gives small grunts, quick smile
		Posture: Moves mechanically to questions or direction, responds to any action with minimal nervous activity, robot-like, practices drills, awaits in line, responds by putting hand up when answering to teacher direction

Cate- gories	Verbal	Nonverbal
8/-18/	**8/**	**18/**
	Predictable student respon- ses that require some measu- re of evaluation, synthesis, and interpretation from the student. The initial beha- vior is in response to tea- cher initiation. Student in- terpretation from teacher in discussed activity. A stu- dent questioning when rela- ted strictly to topic under discussion	**Face:** Look of thinking, pensive, formal expressions **Posture:** Interprets movements, tries to show some arrangement that requires interpretive thinking, works on gymnas- tic routine, test taking, interprets task cards;plays games. Student puts hands in air to give answer to teacher question
9-19	**9**	**19**
	Pupil-initiated talk purely the result of their own ini- tiative and could not be pre- dicted (either positive or negative behavior)	**Face:** Makes interrupting sounds, gasps, sighs **Posture:** Puts hands up in air to ask (unsolicited) question of teacher, gets up and walks around without provocation, begins creative movement education, makes up own ga- mes, makes up own movements, shows initiative in suppor- tive movement, introduces new movements into games not predictable in the ru- les of games
10-20	**10**	**20**
	Confusion, chaos, disorder, noise	**Face:** Silence, children sitting doing nothing, noiselessly awaiting teacher just prior to teacher entry

Table 3.3 - Major CAFIAS Parameters

Major Parameters of CAFIAS	Statistic
Teacher contribution, verbal	%
Teacher contribution, nonverbal	%
Total teacher contribution	%
Student contribution, verbal	%
Student contribution, nonverbal	%
Total student contribution	%
Silence	%
Confusion	%
Total silence and/or confusion	%
Teacher use of questioning, verbal	Ratio
Teacher use of questioning, nonverbal	Ratio
Teacher use of questioning, total	Ratio
Teacher acceptance and praise, verbal	Ratio
Teacher acceptance and praise, nonverbal	Ratio
Teacher acceptance and praise, total	Ratio
Pupil initiation, verbal (Teacher suggestion)	Ratio
Pupil initiation, nonverbal (Teacher suggestion)	Ratio
Pupil initiation, total (Teacher suggestion)	Ratio
Pupil initiation, verbal (Student suggestion)	Ratio
Pupil initiation, nonverbal (Student suggestion)	Ratio
Pupil initiation, total (Student suggestion)	Ratio
Content emphasis (Teacher in-put)	Ratio
Teacher (as teacher)	%
Other students (as teacher)	%
The environment (as teacher)	%
Verbal emphasis	%
Nonverbal emphasis	%
Class structure (as one unit)	%
Class Structure (group or individualized)	%
Class structure (no teacher influence)	%
Teacher empathy to student emotions	Freq. count

sely who is doing the teaching represents a major departure from the Flanders philosophy. Three teaching agencies were considered: the class teacher, the environment, other students. The system is characterized by its flexibility and adaptability.

The study made to determine the validity and reliability of CAFIAS is a fine example of the delicate process needed to determine the validity, or otherwise, of the data gathered.

The performance of the proposed system, the Cheffers Adaptation of the Flanders Interaction Analysis System (CAFIAS) was measured against the performance of FIAS by comparing the scores of trained interpreters answering a questionnaire - Physical Activity Questionnaire. Matrices developed from six carefully selected activity classes were presented to the interpreters who were interpreting the lessons solely from information provided by the matrices ("blind" interpretation), were compared with an outside criteria. The outside criterion consisted of fellow students interpreting the same lessons from information gained by viewing videotapes of these lessons ("live" interpretation). These students were not familiar with either system.

The presence of this "live" interpretation group (control group) enabled measure of face, content and construct validity to be taken and for comparison to be drawn between the scores recorded on the Physical Activity Questionnaire by the two experimental groups.

Inter-observer reliability was determined through comparing the matrices developed for each trained observer.

Thirty-three graduate students were the subjects used in this experiment. Twenty-four of these subjects were taught to code and interpret using both systems. The remaining nine (control group) had not previously contacted either system. Eighteen of the twenty-four trained subjects were randomly assigned to two experimental groups; their task being the "blind" interpretation of physical activity lessons from matrices developed by two main observers. Six volunteers from the training group also coded and developed matrices of the lesson from the videotapes provided; three members used only FIAS and the other three used only CAFIAS. The matrices of these volunteers were then compared with those of the main observers to determine inter-observer agreement correlations.

The following conclusions were substantiated:

1. Observers of physical activity classrooms were more easily able to interpret these behaviors when given a "live" viewing situation than asked to interpret "blind" from matrices developed by either FIAS or CAFIAS.

2. Observers were able to more accurately interpret physical activity classroom behaviors when given a CAFIAS matrix than a FIAS matrix.

A large information can be derived from matrix observation. Figures 3.2 and 3.3 represent the areas of cell emphasis and the interpretations permitted. Figure 3.2 illustrates matrix emphasis for FIAS, whereas do the same thing for CAFIAS. Section A repre-

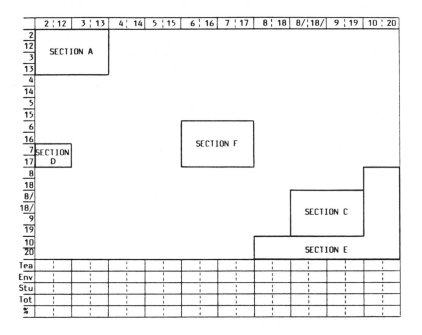

Figure 3.2 — CAFIAS: Matrix interpretation

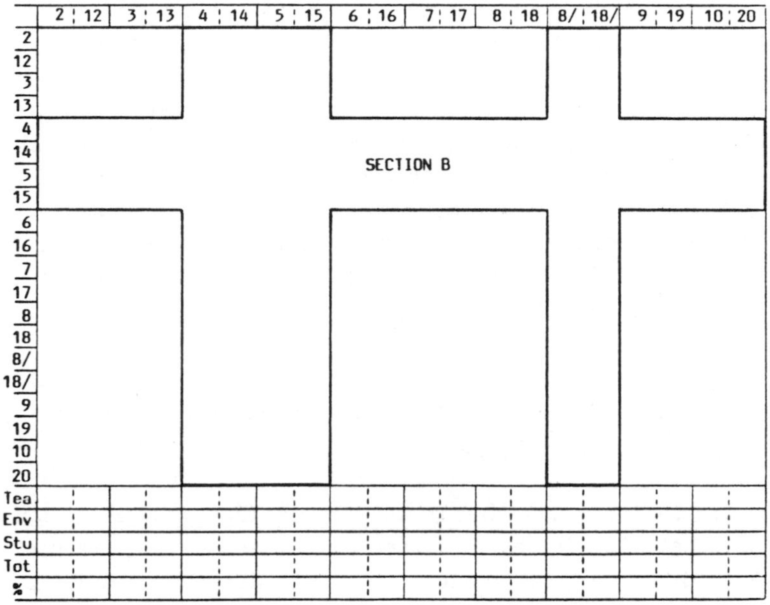

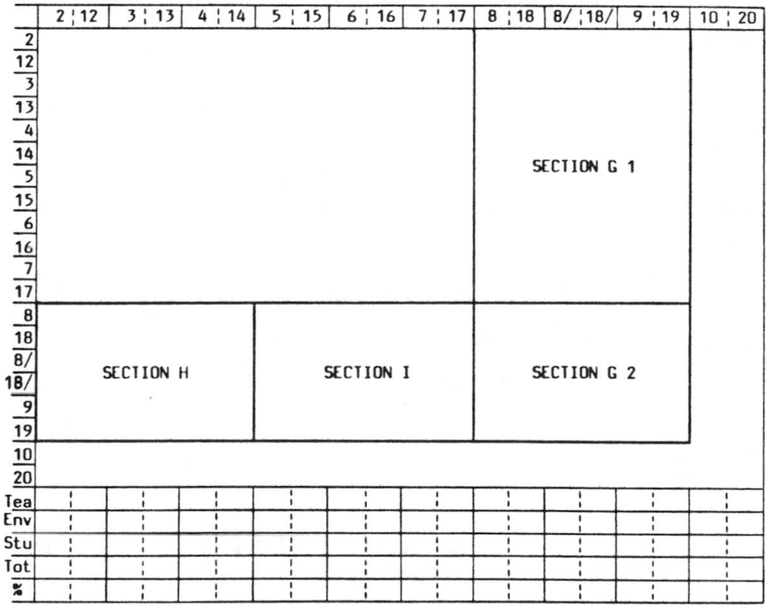

Figure 3.3 - CAFIAS: Matrix interpretation

sents extended teacher acceptance. Section B represents teacher and student emphasis on content. Section C represents continued student initiative resulting from either teacher-suggested or unsolicited student initiative. Section D represents teacher emphasis upon correcting the student with helpful suggestions for improvement. Section E suggests heavy student-to-student inter-action giving and criticism. Emphasis in Section G1 (Figure 3.3) indicates student activity immediately following teacher acti-vity. Section G2 represents extended student behavior. Section H represents teacher indirect response to student activities.

3. Observers asked to interpret "blind" matrices of physical activity lessons using either CAFIAS or FIAS performed more consistently on some types of lessons than on others.

4. CAFIAS as an instrument to describe physical activity classes behavior is reliable when comparison of cell rankings are made indicating the possibility of consistency in cell patter-ning.

5. No advantages were gained in the building of matrices when two coders are used to form a team over matrices developed by individuals.

6. The preparation of non verbal matrices by observers working exclusively on the non verbal dimensions were not as accurate in representing classroom behaviors as observers viewing lessons under both verbal and non verbal dimensions.

Box 3.2 - INTERACTION ANALYSIS: Instruments of observation and
Methods of gathering data

INSTRUMENTS

(Che,73)   Cheffers Adaptation of Flanders Interaction
              Analysis System (CAFIAS)
              6 Cl, 33 Obs
              Face, content and construct validity, reliability

(Hei,80)   Physical Education Interaction Analysis
(Hei,83)   Categories (PEIAC/LH-75)
            Multidimensional system: T & S talk Social access,
            activity/passivity, Social form (organization and
            tasks)
            24 Less, 6 Obs, video
            Discriminative analysis

(Lun,74)   6 experts, 10 tapes, multidimensional system
            choreography
            Reliability, objectivity, construct & content
            validity

(Mos,72)   Modification of FIAS
            10 ST, second,
            Interobserver reliability

(Ols,79)   Observational System for Instructional Analysis
            Physical Education (OSIA-PE)
            12 Cl, video
            Inter- and intra-Observer reliability

(P&D,77b)   Observational System for the Analysis of Classroom
            Instruction (Hough, 1966)
            3 Obs, ST, second,
            Reliability (W Kendall, Anova)

(Spl,79)   Physical Education Interaction Analysis System
            (PEIAC)
            4 T (M), 8 Less/T, second
            Teaching style (Direct vs Indirect)
            Inter- and intra-observer variance.

(Tay,79)   Physical education observation Intrument
            Description, validity, reliability

FIELD STUDIES: Design of studies, methods of gathering data, contexts

----

(Akk,79)   B ST, JHS, PEIAC/LH75
                Indoor activities
                Indirect vs direct teaching

(All,79)   10 Cl, 5 T, 316 S, JHS, video, ITBAS
                S gender, T perception of S level of participation

(Bah,71)   42 T (21 M 21 W), FIAS
                California Psychological Inventory
                Presage - Process

(Bat,75)   T, elem, CAFIAS
                English, Math, Physical Education
                Comparison of predicted and actual behaviors

(Ben,77)   30 ST, SAFIAS
                MTAI, T behaviors, California T scale
                Presage - Process - Environment: urban, suburban

(Boo,67)   9 T (W), 36 S, JHS, mod. OScAR
(Boo,66)   Factor analysis

(Bro,80)   12 T (6M, 6W), Brown Dyadic IA instrument
                Sex of T, sex of S, T perceived skill of S,
                Status of S as an athlete or non-athlete

(C&M,78)   83 Cl, CAFIAS, video
                Various subject matters
                Descriptive study

(Cou,76)   31 T (19 exp, 12 cont), SAFIAS
                pre and post training obs
                Teaching styles
                Presage process: MTAI, SAFIAS, PCI

(D&S,77)   3 T, 20 Less, Didactic IA
                Gymnastics
                Descriptive

(Dou,70)   3 T, 6 Cl, 115 S, mod. FIAS
              Teaching styles (command, task, individual)

(Ewe,81)   2 T, 4 Cl, elem (1 adapt), FIAS
              Grade level, normal vs adapted

(Gau,80)   4 T, 4 Cl (gr2), mainstreamed, Audio, OSIA-PE
              Handicaped vs Normal children

(Imw,84)   12 ST (6 M - 6 W) - CAFIAS
              Basketball instructional period (15 min)
              Exp vs Cont - Planning vs non planning groups

(Kas,74)   3 (T & Head varsity athletic C)
              Univ level, Mod. FIAS
              Comparison of T & C

(Lew,74)   25 ST (M), FIAS
              Teaching Stiuation Reaction Test, S Perception of
              T influence
              Presage - Process

(Lew,79)   2 Cl, ST, 6 Less, live, VICS-M
              Styles of teaching

(Lom,79)   4 T, elem, CAFIAS

(L&C,83)   Variability of teaching behaviors
              Time of the day, day of the week, content of the
              lesson, mode of supervision by T

(Lom,82)   4 T, CAFIAS
              Same subjects as in (Lom,79)
              Longitudinal study - intra-individual variability

(Lor,82)   2 T (W), univ, Modif. Joyce system
              Dance
              Descriptive data

(Luc,78a)   8 T, 21 Class, video, Hough 1966
               Various subject matters (Conceptual approach)
               Descriptive data

(Lyd,78)   285 S, CAFIAS
               Schilling Body Coordination Test, Martinek -
               Zaichkovsky Self Concept scale
               Gender, grade, ethnic groups, style of teaching
               decision making

(M,C,Z,76)   505 S, elem, video, CAFIAS
(Man,74)   Decision making

(Man,83)   30 T, 60 Cl, video, CAFIAS, ALT-PE
               Maslach Burnout Inventory (MBI)
               Comparison of 10 randomly T selected in low-
               burnout and high burn-out groups

(M&K,84)   3 T, 128 ST, K3, CAFIAS
               Teacher Expectations, Physical Attractiveness
               Multivariate analysis

(Maw,77)   24 S, elem, CAFIAS
               Movement education
               Adapted vs regular Classes

(Maws,73)   31 ST, 28 CT, 3 Supervisors, elem & second
               VICS (Verbal Category System)
               Variations of teaching IA during 8 weeks
               Teaching program
(Mel,71)   10 T, FIAS
               California T scale, Objectives (Bloom, Krathwohl)
               Presage - Process

(Mor,78a)   40 Cl, 20 elem, 20 second, video
(Mor,78b)   Bellack System of observation
               Various subject matter
               Descriptive data

(Nyg,71)   40 T (21 F, 19 M)
(Nyg,75)   elem to univ, audio-FIAS
               gender, school level

(Nyg,78)   24 T, audio, FIAS
Various subject matters
Perceived and actual IA according to T experience

(Ols,82)   24 Cl, elem, JHS, SHS, (8 each level)
(Ols,83b)   Various subject matter
Descriptive

(P&D,77a)   8 ST (W), live, Hough System (1966)
Various subject matters
Descriptive

(Pie,78)   30 ST, live, Hough (1966)
Track and field, gymnastics, team sports
gender, subject matter

(Ran,75)   42 ST, elem, RIAS
Gender, grade level, personality characteristics
(dominance or submissiveness)

(R,S,T,82)   12 T, 44 observation periods, 8-13 Year old S,
RIAS
Gymnastics, swimming
Gender, S age, subject matter

(Rep,79)   44 Classes (14 M, 30 W) ST, Videotapes,
PEIAC/LH-75
Presage - Process, personality inventory -
teaching behaviours

(S,C,Z,83)   6 T, 208 S, 1 to 5th grades, CAFIAS, Cheffers &
(Sch,82)   Mancini Human movement attitude scale,
Minnesota tests of creative thinking, Johnson
Fundamental Skill Tests, Martinek - Zaichkovsky
Self-concept scale
Comparison according to decision making by S

(Tav,77)   4 T (M), 8 Less, JHS, PEIAS
Descriptive study

(Twa,79)   16 T (8 M, 8 W), elem, RIAS
               Gender, grade level

(Und,78)   1 T, 1 Cl, 38 s, *(Und,79)
               Basket ball
               Descriptive

(Und,80)   1 T, 2 Class, 11 year old boys, *(Und,79)
               Comparison of teaching styles

(Wue,82)   2 T, 2 ST, 2 Less/T, video, CAFIAS, IRG 2
               Self report of emotional intensity, involvement,
               heart rate

PICTURE OF TEACHING RELATIONSHIP THROUGH TEACHER - STUDENT INTERACTION ANALYSIS.

In one of the first descriptive studies in physical education teaching, Nygaard (1971, 1975) observed 40 teachers at different levels, from elementary to college level. In the teacher's categories, the indirect influence was largely predominant, exceeding 70 %. This was exhibited by extremely low indirect/direct (I/D) ratios obtained, and by the very low student talk/teacher talk (ST/TT) ratios obtained. The indirect influence was lower than 10 %. This tendency was more accentuated in men than in women. This predominant role of direct influence has been confirmed by Cheffers (1973), Cheffers & Mancini (1978), Piéron & Drion (1977) and by Brunelle (1973), in using different systems of observation. The talk starts overwhelmingly from the teacher: approximately 80 % for the teacher and less than 10 % for the pupil. This observation was more strongly illustrated in men than in women. It was also concluded that the teacher was more content centered that student centered (Nygaard, 1971, 1975).

Cheffers and Mancini (1978) observed the 83 lessons recorded in the Video Data Bank (Anderson, 1975). They confirmed previous data gathered by the original FIAS that predominant teacher behaviors were lecture and direction giving. Very little teacher praise, acceptance of students feelings and ideas, teacher questionning occurred in these lessons.

Studies of teacher - student interaction can be organized like in other sections in this report according to context variables (gender, school or grade level) and programme variables (methodologies).

VARIATIONS ACCORDING TO CONTEXT VARIABLES.

GENDER. The question to be answered is: do male and female teachers differ from each other in their verbal and/or non verbal communication? The answer seems to be that minimal differences must be expected in interaction parameters, category usage, and in interaction patterns between male and female teachers. When differences are observed they showed very little consistency from one study to another.

In his study on 40 teachers, Nygaard (1975) observed that both male and female teachers were direct verbal influences, with the male teachers more direct overall. The female teachers encouraged more student talk in comparison to teacher talk than did the male teachers. It was of interest to note that despite the presence of a higher I/D ratio, indicating a less direct verbal influence, the female teacher most frequently used a verbal pattern that was more autocratic or command-like than the verbal pattern most frequently used by male teachers, but at the same time used significantly less lecture than did the male teachers. Cheffers & Mancini (1978) concluded that elementary male teachers put more emphasis on content than elementary female teachers. Contrary to the Nygaard's study, Cheffers & Mancini concluded that differences between male and female teachers were low and generally non significant as far as category use was concerned.

Rankin (1975) reported that from thirty comparisons using ANOVA, only three were statistically significant. Female student teachers used more gestures than their male counterparts.

SCHOOL OR GRADE LEVEL. As in the comparison between sexes, minimal differences existed in interaction parameters, in category usage, and in interaction patterns between elementary and secondary teachers. The most direct verbal influence was exerted by the high school physical education teachers, the least by the lower and upper elementary teachers (Nygaard, 1975). More emphasis was placed on content at the secondary level than at the elementary level (Cheffers & Mancini, 1978).

Using the Rankin Interaction Analysis System (RIAS), Twa (1979) concluded that the most striking finding of his study was the remarkable similarity of teacher behavior at the primary and intermediate level. It appears from these results that elementary physical education teachers teach primary and intermediate classes the same, at least within the limits of the ten behaviors described by the Rankin Interaction Analysis System.

Twa (1979) found only two significant differences involving sex of the teacher and grade level. Male teachers praised more at the primary level than at the intermediate level, whereas the female teachers praised more at the intermediate level than at the elementary level.

NORMAL VS ADAPTED OR MAINSTREAMED CLASSES. Mawdsley (1977) compared teacher behaviors in regular and adapted movement classes. Teachers seemed to utilize similar behaviors and interaction patterns in both classes. Except for a high proportion of student behaviors when females are teaching, male and female teachers do not differ in how they behave, interact and relate to students in both adapted and regular classes.

Gauthier (1980) observed by means of the Observation System Instructional Activities in Physical Education (OSIA-physical education) four mainstreamed second grade classes taught by male physical education teachers. Results of the multivariate analysis of variance indicated that there was no significant overall difference in teacher-student interaction between handicaped and normal pupils. Only two variables differed significantly: handicaped pupils received more positive feedback and less feedback following a movement response than normal children.

VARIATIONS ACCORDING TO PROGRAMME VARIABLES.

DECISION MAKING. Methodologies were verified by using the interaction analysis systems. Mancini, Cheffers & Zaichkovsky (1976) compared interaction in human movement classes in which the teachers made all the decisions with classes (TDMA) in which students shared some part in the decision making process (CDMA). In the CDMA groups, the children were permitted to make the following decisions: choice of apparatus, choice and sequence of activity at each apparatus, choice of whether or not to take part in activities, choice of time allocation throughout the period.

In the TDMA groups, teachers talked more and contributed more to class behaviors than in CDMA groups. In CDMA groups, students talked more, contributed more to class behaviors, student initiated behaviors were greater than in the TDMA groups. in CDMA groups, teachers used questions rather than lecture to stress lesson content, they were more indirect than in the TDMA group.

Non verbal contributions of teacher and students, and emphasis on content were the same across groups (Mancini, Cheffers & Zaichkovsky, 1976).

There were several similarities in a study by Lydon & Cheffers (1984). The two variable decision-making teaching models were designated as the Vertical Teaching Model (close to TDMA) and the Horizontal Teaching Model (CDMA). During the Horizontal Teaching, the teacher used more questionning, displayed more non verbal response, and allowed more student initiated response to occur.

Other variables were used in comparing TDMA and CDMA groups. They were gathered through attitude scales, self concept measures, motor skill tests and creativity measures. Schempp, Cheffers & Zaichkovsky (1983) found that all the measures were in favor of the groups wherein the decision making process was shared by teacher and students. However, it seems premature to conclude that a consistent general trend supported philosophies and theories advocating a class environment which allow a degree of student autonomy. Other studies (Lydon, 1978; Lynch, 1980) did not show the same differences in favor of the CDMA groups. The question remains largely unanswered.

TEACHING STYLES. FIAS or adapted systems were frequently utilized to study the effect on interaction of the different teaching style advocated in the Mosston's spectrum of teaching styles (Countiss, 1976; Dougherty, 1970; Jacoby, 1975).

Teacher-Student Interaction

A study by Lewis (1979) was conducted to determine if self coded feedback from Verbal Interaction Category System - Modified (VICS-M), a modification of the Verbal Interaction Category System (VICS) by Amidon & Hunter would help physical education students understand and control specific patterns of verbal behavior, specifically three of Muska Mosston's Spectrum of Teaching Styles-command, guided discovery and problem solving.

JOB SATISFACTION.

Job satisaction could exert a strong influence on the interaction and on the other hand discipline problems and a poor interaction could decrease job satisfaction.

Mancini, Wuest, Clark & Ridosh (1983) compared interaction of low and high burnout secondary physical education teachers. Key syndrome of the burnout is emotional exhaustion, development of negative or impersonal feelings and attitudes over pupils, and a tendency to evaluate one's job performance negatively.

Thirty physical education teachers were distributed in two groups according to the Maslach Burnout Inventory. In this study, interaction was observed through the CAFIAS instrument; student involvement was investigated by the ALT-Physical Education instrument.

Findings showed that low burnout teachers were more varied in their teaching behaviors. They gave more praise and exhibited more acceptance of their students'ideas and feelings. They interacted more frequently with their students.

THE EXPECTANCY PHENOMENON IN TEACHER - STUDENT INTERACTION.

The Dyadic Adaptation of Cheffers adaptation of Flanders Interaction Analysis System (DAC) was developed to describe the interaction between the teacher and a particular student. In DAC, the emphasis is placed on the word dyadic. When a teacher directs a behavior to a student, the observer codes the interaction between them. The observer does not code behaviors toward the entire class or to large groups.

This adaptation was successfully applied in a consistent effort to investigate the expectancy phenomenon (Pygmalyon effect) occurring in a class.

Pygmalion theory basically explains the phenomenon of the self-fulfilling prophecy in which students perform in accordance with expectations of their teachers. Martinek (1983) refers to "Galatea" or "Golem" effects in physical education.

> "Galatea effects occur when there is a positive effect from the teacher's expectations. In other words, if the teacher expects a particular student to perform well and begins acting toward that student accordingly, these biased interactions may well result in superior student performance. Likewise, Golem effects occur when a teacher expects a particular student to be a low achiever and behaves accordingly toward that student." (Martinek, 1983, p. 59).

In classroom teaching several experiences showed that some differences in behaviors could be expected from teachers in their interactions with students according to their perceptions of student skills. Good & Brophy (1978) reported minor differences in the frequency of teacher contacts with pupils of different achievement levels. They found more important variations in the quality of these contacts.

In physical education teaching, the expectancy phenomenon has been studied by means of interaction analysis, especially by a dyadic version of CAFIAS in elementary classes and in mainstreamed classes (Martinek & Johnson, 1979; Martinek & Karper, 1981). Differences were evidenced in encouragement, acceptance of ideas and questioning, according to teachers expectations. All these variables are not necessarily strongly related with teaching effectiveness.

In a study by Martinek & Johnson (1979) the DAC was used to describe teacher expectations on teacher-student interaction. On a total of 100 students, the authors observed the interaction with the highest 10 and lowest 10 according to ratings by their teacher according to how they were expected to perform in terms of physical achievement. Several findings tended to confirm the expectancy phenomenon. Expected high achievers received significantly more contacts from the teacher, more praise and encouragement than expected low achievers. The teachers' acceptance and use of student ideas were greater in the high expectancy group. The teachers tended to more readily accept and utilize actions and ideas of high expectancy pupils. Another significant difference was observed in favour of the expected high achivers, in "analytic student response".

The students physical attractiveness exerts an influence on teacher expectations and on several aspects of teacher-student interaction. Martinek (1981) observed two elementary physical education classes taught by females teachers. In the study, 30 graduate students were asked to rate 141 children from a black and white photo of each child. A total of 100 students, from the upper and lower thirds in each class for both teachers, comprised the sample. The teachers rated their students on the following variables: (1) overall performance in physical skill; (2) social relations with peers; (3) cooperative behavior during class; (4) ability to reason. It was assumed that attractive student were perceived as potentially better performers and more socially integrative.

The data analysis of dyadic interactions suggests that "differential behavior among the teachers and high and low attractive groups was found to be unique for one of the CAFIAS variables: teacher acceptance and use of the students'ideas. Specifically, it was found that the ideas and actions of the high attractive sixth grades students were more frequently accepted and used by the teachers than were low attractive students".

Martinek and Karper (1981) described the differences of handicaped and non-handicaped children in mainstreamed physical education classes in terms of the teachers' expectation for their physical performance, social relations, cooperative behavior and ability to reason during physical education instruction. The teachers had significantly lower expectations for the handicapped students social relation with peers than the non-handicaped.

The expectancy phenomenon was not fully confirmed by data collected by Piéron (1982b) and by Piéron & Forceille (1983). Teachers behaved approximately in the same way with low achievers than with high achievers. Teachers tended to react more frequently to low achievers unsuccessful trials. These students were provided with more frequent feedback and encouragement. Nevertheless the size of the distinction in teacher interventions with low achievers did not seem to be sufficiently high to compensate the differences evidenced in the motor engagement time or success rate variables.

The dyadic interactive events occuring in a class must be looked at very carefully. Many teacher behaviors included in the interactive events, like augmented feedback and praise, are considered as enthusiastic behaviors by students in physical education teaching (Caruso, 1980). More striking is the fact that many non interactive events are clearly designated as unenthusiastic behaviors, and considered as disinterest, withdrawal from the group, or detachment (Caruso, 1980).

TEACHING PATTERNS.

A teaching act is not an isolated action. It has its origin and a consequence. Teachers interventions are determined by their planning, by their perception of what is happening in the class, by students behaviors, and by immediate reactions to these behaviors. Although these remarks seem self evident, relatively few data exist concerning the sequence of events occuring in a physical education class.

One of the main reasons for reconstructing the chain of events will be to estimate the probability or previsibility of occurence of various teaching events in the class environment.

OBSERVATION INSTRUMENTS.

Several instruments or procedures contribute to the identification of the sequence:

(1) Flanders (1970) described a procedure permetting a reconstruction of this sequence for the interaction matrix. The matrix is built in such a way that what is immediately preceding or following the occurence of an event can always be identified. Authors using the FIAS or its adaptations usually draw patterns

from their data. Studies using CAFIAS usually describe the interaction patterns. These patterns are built in a slightly different
manner than the description made by Flanders.

(2) The observation system of Bellack is based on "pedagogical moves" and articulated around categories labeled "structuring, soliciting, responding and reacting". The system is particularly well adapted to describe teaching sequences. After a
first adaptation, not always very conclusive according to reliability by Hupé (1974) the observation schedule was revised and
applied to 40 classes from the Video Data Bank tapes by Morgenegg
(1978b). Twenty were from the elementary grades and 20 from the
high school grades.

(3) Olson (1979) developed from the Observational System for
Instructional Analysis (OSIA), an instrument specifically devised
to observe the teaching sequence of events. The instrument is
used to distinguish behaviors related to instructional events,
teaching strategies and styles, and learner events. Events may be
coded on seven dimensions simultaneously: 1. focus of observation
(teacher, student, setting); 2. instructional situation, organization, setting; 3. source of instructional events; 4. instructional functions and categories; 5. sub-categories of instructional functions; 6. communication modes; 7. specific subscripted
events.

GENERAL INTERACTION PATTERNS.

The analysis by Nygaard (1975) provides researchers with a
general picture of the verbal interaction pattern. It is based on
the observation of 40 male and female teachers.

The primary interaction pattern is based on the sequence of
the following categories: "lecture - silence and/or confusion -
lecture" or "lecture - silence and/or confusion - direction -
silence and/or confusion - lecture". A secondary pattern was
identified as "lecture - asking questions - student talk -
lecture".

It is evident that these patterns identified through FIAS are unsatisfactory in identifying such students non verbal activity as silence and/or confusion.

Piéron & Drion (1977) used the observational system for the analysis of classroom interaction (Hough, 1967) and described a pattern including demonstration and students activity in the sequence: "students activity - lecture - demonstration - direction - student activity".

In the Morgenegg study (1978a, 1978b), teaching cycles starting from the teacher were 50 % accounted for by the "SOL,RES" cycle (sollicitation and response). Five cycles represented almost 95 % of the all the cycles starting from the teacher. Cycles initiated by students proved to be more varied. The most frequent cycle is also the "SOL,RES" (more than 40 %). Let us point out that 88.9 % were teacher initiated and 11.1 % student initiated.

Morgenegg (1978b) summarized his results according to two lists of statements: one pertaining to the teacher, the other to pupils. Pertaining to the teacher:

"1. The most active player in the gymnasium is the teacher. The teacher executes almost two thirds of all combined moves for teacher and pupils. The dominant moves used by the teacher are soliciting (39.8 %) and reacting (15.7 %). 2. All teacher moves are short (2-3 seconds) except structuring which average 12 seconds. 3. Teachers use direct soliciting five times more frequently than indirect soliciting. 4. Teachers use positive reacting on a 2:1 ratio to negative reacting. 5. Eighty-nine percent of all cycles are initiated by teachers. 6. Interchange of pedagogical moves between teacher and pupils is generally very short, i.e. one or two moves. 7. Substantive meaning dominates the teacher moves. 8. Verbal mode is used principally for communicating the pedagogical moves. 9. In general, structuring moves are directed to the class, while solliciting moves are directed to individuals.

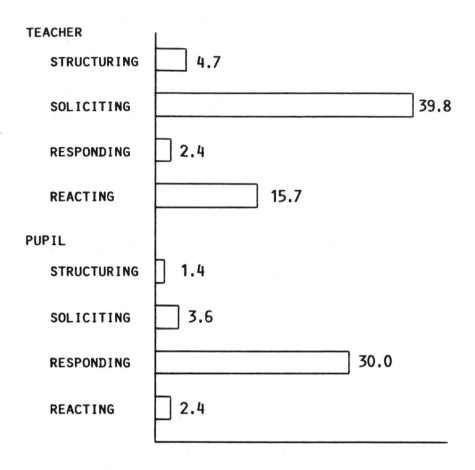

Figure 3.4 - Percent distribution of pedagogical moves for teachers and pupils (Morgenegg, 1978b).

Pertaining to pupils:

1. The pupils'dominant role is responding to the teacher's solicitations. 2. Pupils' responses are, for the most part, non verbal. 3. Pupils use indirect solicitations on a 15:1 ratio to direct solicitations. 4. Pupils initiate 11 % of all cycles. 5. Over half of all pupil initiated interaction units are only 2 moves in length. 6. When pupils react, it is in a neutral from, rather than a positive or negative form."

Teacher-Student Interaction

In her analysis of 24 lessons at different teaching levels, Olson (1982) identified three and four elements sequences. 84 % included three elements and 16 % included four elements.

The following sequence of events: "Teacher initiation - Teacher solicitation - Student response" was identified as the most frequent sequence. The most frequent four elements sequence was "Teacher solicitation - Student response - Teacher initiation - Teacher solicitation".

VARIATIONS ACCORDING TO CONTEXT: Gender and school level.

"Similar patterns were exhibited when the total female and total male matrices were examined. For the 21 female teachers, the most frequently occurring verbal interaction pattern was a 5-10-6-10-5 pattern, that is lecture, followed by silence or confusion, followed by commands or direction, followed by silence or confusion, followed by lecture. For the 19 male teachers, the most frequently occurring verbal interaction pattern was a 5-4-8-3-5 pattern. This pattern indicatedextended periods of lecture followed by questions to which student-talk response occurred, followed by acceptance or use of student ideas and then lecture" (Nygaard, 1975, p. 355).

The primary teaching patterns of secondary male and female teachers were identical (Table 3.4).

Cheffers et Mancini (1978) concluded from their analysis of the 83 lessons of the Video Data Bank that the patterns observed in the elementary classes were remarkably similar, and reflect a predominance of teacher information giving along with directions and predictable student responses; there was little student initiation. When student initiation was evident, it tended to take place among students, not between students and teacher(s). At all times, however, the student behaviors occured as a result of initial teacher suggestion.

In the secondary lessons, teacher emphasis on information giving, directing and student predictable responses again predominated. Direct connection with student extended skill practice or game practice was detected. Again, student behavior resulted from initial teacher suggestion.

Table 3.4 - Patterns of interaction (Cheffers & Mancini, 1978).

ELEMENTARY

Male: (1) Extended teacher information giving and demonstration, followed by narrow student response, leading to more teacher information giving, to extended teacher direction giving and more narrow student response.

(2) Student playing games with other students.

Female: (1) Extended teacher information giving, followed by narrow student response, followed by more teacher directions.

(2) Extended drills, followed by extended games, followed by teacher information giving.

SECONDARY

Games being played on an extended note, followed by extended teacher information giving, then teacher directions, narrow student response, followed by more teacher directions.

Morgenegg (1978b) observed like Cheffers and Mancini that teacher-pupil interchanges were remarkably similar across grade levels, for both teachers and pupils. The few exceptions were: 1. Elementary pupils structure slightly more than secondary pupils. 2. Elementary teachers react positively almost twice as frequently as secondary teachers.

The similarity of teaching behavior patterns across age and sex were also observed by Twa (1979) using the Rankin Interaction Analysis System. The pattern was as follows "Teacher talk followed by Student movement - Teacher talk - Teacher gestures - Teacher talk". It accounted for 45 % of the total behaviors exhibited in the classes (male and female primary and intermediate elementary classes).

TEACHING METHODOLOGY.

The approach used by the teacher exerts a stronger influence on the teaching pattern than the age or sex of the participants. In classes where the teacher takes all the decisions, the pattern was: teacher lecturing and giving directions to students who respond with predictable non verbal activity. In classes where the teacher shared some decisions with the students, the pattern was quite different: teacher giving information (lecturing) and asking questions followed by students who respond with predictable and analytical verbal and non verbal behavior which was praised and accepted by the teacher (Lydon, 1978; Schempp, Cheffers & Zaichkovsky, 1983).

CHAPTER 4

STUDENT BEHAVIOR

The analysis of teaching aims at providing an objective picture of what is happening in the gymnasium. Studying the students behaviors has been a strong component of descriptive studies.

In physical education, one cannot guess pupil learning gains by relying only on teacher interventions. Recently, researchers have moved from a primary concern with teacher behaviors to other instructional variables, especially pupil variables. Everyone realizes that interaction is a two-way phenomenon. It is clear that the pupils ability and behaviors influence interactions and therefore are associated with teaching behaviors.

Studies based on pupil observation gained some momentum from trends in classroom teacher effectiveness research. Pupil activities are central to their learning. They are viewed as the mediating link to learning. The total amount of active learning time in a particular motor skill seems to be the most important determinant of pupil achievement at that motor skill.

Through student observation, through their behaviors, their expressed attitudes, values and observable changes, it is hoped to better appraise education outcomes and the extent of teacher's influence.

INSTRUMENTS OF OBSERVATION.

Several approaches have been used to describe the pupils' behaviors and engagement: (1) considering the activity of the whole class; (2) analyzing the activities and behaviors of selected target pupils (choosen randomly or selected according to various criteria).

THE ACTIVITY OF THE WHOLE CLASS. Siedentop (1976) used a technique labeled Placheck (Planned activity check) consisting in a quick scanning of the class and a count of the number of pupils engaged in a specific behavior. The placheck provides a gross indication of whether the pupils are engaged in motor activities or/and whether they are doing what they are expected to do. This technique was used in several studies of behavior modification to control some side effects of the program (Hamilton, 1974; Boehm, 1974). These authors observed the proportions of students engaged in appropriate or inappropriate behaviors (Rife, 1973). A placheck is done at regular time intervals. The same technique is described by Anderson (1980) as "spot checking".

In another series of studies at the Ohio State University, class climate is determined according to the involvement of the majority of the class: motor activity, waiting, information receiving or managerial activities (Stewart, 1977; Freedman, 1978). This measure seems rather inaccurate. The labeling of "class climate" could be confused with the current "class climate" concept used in studies of the teaching process like in Dunkin & Biddle's review of literature (1974).

INDIVIDUAL BEHAVIORS. A second approach consisted of developing specific observational systems based on students behaviors in choosing a target pupil and in observing systematically his/her behaviors.

Several instruments are directly linked to the concept of engaged time or motor activity of the student: BESTPED (Laubach, 1975; Costello & Laubach, 1978; Borys, 1983), ALT-PE (Siedentop, Birdwell & Metzler, 1979), OBEL/ULg (Piéron & Haan, 1980; Piéron & Dohogne, 1980; Piéron & Cloes, 1981). Cheffers, Brunelle & Von Kelsch (1980) have developed a different type of instrument focusing on the student involvement in the activities.

A brief description of these instruments seems to be useful:

(1) BESTPED, an acronym for BEhavior of STudents in Physical Education has been developed by Laubach (1975) and applied in the framework of the Video Data Bank to analyze the behaviors of 193 students selected in 20 elementary and secondary school classes. It served in a study whose objective was to increase the motor engagement time (Borys, 1983).

(2) OBEL/ULG presents several analogies with the BESTPED system. Its distinct originality lies in taking note of teacher's interventions towards the target student under observation. It was mostly used in comparing classes managed by master teachers and student teachers, in comparing student behaviors according to the subject matter taught (Piéron & Haan, 1980; Piéron & Dohogne, 1980, Piéron & Cloes, 1981).

Table 4.1 - BESTPED System: Categories in function and Mode Dimension (Laubach, 1974; Costello & Laubach, 1978).

FUNCTION DIMENSION

    Practice
    Game Playing
    Exercise
    Explore
    Express-Communicate
    Position
    Equip
    Assist
    Receive Information
    Give Information
    Await
    Diverge
    Off Monitor

MODE DIMENSION
    Movement
    Non-Movement

---

(3) ALT-PE (Academic Learning Time - Physical Education) has been developed from Berliner's contention that teacher behavior does not impact directly on students achievement, but instead impact indirectly through decreasing or increasing students engagement on task. ALT-PE has been adapted to physical education by Siedentop, Birdwell & Metzler (1979) and refined after by Siedentop, Tousignant & Parker (1982).

Inspired by the Beginning Teacher Evaluation Study research program, Siedentop, Birdwell & Metzler (1979) adapted to physical education teaching the variable labeled Academic Learning Time (ALT) and made it more specific with ALT(PE)-M. It was defined as the portion of engaged time in which the pupil is performing a motor task at a low error rate. The ALT is used with the under-

Table 4.2 - OBEL/ULg System: Categories in student behavior and teacher behavior dimensions (Piéron & Cloes, 1981).

STUDENT BEHAVIOR DIMENSION

Motor Activity (Engaged Time)
Managerial Tasks
Receiving Information
Waiting
Verbal Interactions (with the Teacher)
Verbal Interactions (with other Students)
Off-Task Behaviors
Various

TEACHER BEHAVIOR DIMENSION

Instruction
Organization
Feedback
Affectivity
Silent Observation
Various

---

lying assumption that the accrual of motor engagement time is related to improved pupil achievement. From Siedentop's perspective, when achievement is difficult to measure as for some physical education learning objectives, motor engagement time or ALT becomes a legitimate substitute for pupils achievement. The constructed variable of ALT stands between measures of teaching and measures of student learning gains.

ALT has several dimensions. Observers are requested to make decisions regarding each of its dimension: (1) general content or subject matter content; (2) subject matter is subdivided in knowledge or motor content; (3) nature of student response.

Table 4.3 - Academic Learning Time - Physical Education (Siedentop, Tousignant & Parker, 1982).

CONTENT LEVEL

General content	Subject matter knowledge	Subject matter motor
Transition	Technique	Skill practice
Management	Strategy	Scrimmage/Routine
Break	Rules	Game
Warm up	Social behavior	Fitness
	Background	

LEARNER INVOLVEMENT LEVEL

Not motor engaged	Motor engaged
Interim	Motor appropriate
Waiting	Motor inappropriate
Off-task	Supporting
Cognitive	

"An interesting corollary to the work on controlled practice is the current research at the Far West Lab on the error rate of children's work. These results show that students make the most progress when they spend time on work in which they have a low error rate, or when their time is balanced between a low error rate and a moderate error rate" (Rosenshine, 1978).

The difficulty in ALT categorizing could be to decide whether learner engagement in task relevant activities is hard, medium or easy.

In ALT-PE I (Siedentop, Metzler & Birdwell, 1979), the observer must make decisions according to four major dimensions: the setting, the content, the learner moves and the difficulty level of the task.

ALT-PE II (Siedentop, Tousignant & Parker, 1982) modified the initial system in view to spend less time making decisions during each observation interval. The second version appears to place higher priority on what the students are doing regardless of what the teacher is doing.

Rife, Shute & Dodds (1985) compared videotapes of two university instructors and students in coeducational classes of volleyball and badminton (36 students and 18 students respectively) in view to answer questions about the comparability of data collected by these two observation schedules.

"What information is excluded?
Do these two versions provide a similar enough picture of the gymnasium so there is no problem shifting from version I to version II ?" (Rife, Shute & Dodds, 1985).

Results showed that the two versions provide similar information about students' opportunities to learn physical education skills, each system has some small advantages over the other.

Either version can be a useful and appropriate research instrument depending on the research questions investigated. Shifting from one version to the other can be made quickly with properly supervised practice and appropriate feedback.

ALT-PE has provoked an important movement of study. It has been used in different settings, in descriptive analytic studies, intervention studies and in process product studies. The rationale and concepts have been largely explained by Metzler (1982), and in the Journal of Teaching in Physical Education monograph "Time To Learn In Physical Education. History, Completed Research, and Potential Future for Academic Learning Time in Physical Education" (Dodds & Rife, 1983). The monograph shows the popularity and range of application of the ALT-PE, it provides insights about the accumulated data base, critiques shortcomings of recent research efforts, and offers suggestion for future research and applications (Alexander, 1983; Anderson, 1983b; Aufderheide, 1983; Griffey, 1983a; Hawkins, Wiegand & Bahneman, 1983; Martinek & Karper, 1983; Metzler, 1983c; Parker & O'Sullivan, 1983; Siedentop, 1983b; Templin, 1983; Tousignant, Brunelle, Piéron & Dhillon, 1983). Several results were summarized by Dodds, Rife & Metzler (1982).

Table 4.4 - Individual Reaction Gestalt, Third Edition (IRG III).

Code verbal	non verbal	Category	Description	Concepts
1	11	No apparent involvement	Wandering around the learning area doing something else not on task	Low involvement
2	12	Distracted involvement	Present, but not giving the lesson concentration. Talking to someone	Low involvement
3	13	Spasmodic involvement	No permanent focus. Fluctuates on and off task	Spasmodic involvement
4	14	Engrossed	Permanent focus. No apparent emotional release. Eyes never leaving the task	Engrossed involved

Primary subscripts:

5 : **Where** there is strong emotion, laughing, smiling, frowning but the behaviors are in control.

6 : Where there is excessive emotional release positive or negative, and where the behaviors are observed to be out of control, e.g. hugging, jumping up and down yelling.

V : Where physical violence is occurring.

N : Where observably negative behaviors are being used

G : Where the individual is interacting in a group.

(4) Telama et al. (1982) combined the observation of students behavior with other observations of teacher behavior and with different questionnaires assessing other aspects of the teaching process. Categories used in observing the student are close to those used in BESTPED or OBEL/ULg.

(5) IRG II was developed by Cheffers, Brunelle & Von Kelsch (1980) to measure the degree of involvement of an individual or a group in a large variety of settings. Involvement is described on a continuum of intensity ranging from low, no apparent involvement to high, intense and uncontrolled emotional involvement. Six behavioral categories comprise the continuum; the degree of involvement can also be viewed in terms of three concepts; low involvement, spasmodic involvement and intense involvement. The development of IRG III resulted from the use and validation procedures with IRG II (Cheffers, Wuest & Crowley, 1981). The number of categories was now reduced from six to four with emotionality added as a subscript after the first four categories. It was realized that emotionality could accompany students uninvolved as well as those who were engrossed with the task in hand. The greater versatility added a greater sensitivity to the description of task behaviors as well. It appears that the process of instrument refinement must continue if pedagogy is to gain credibility in the world of science. Too often single, one-time instruments are used to provide precious data in a field that has not distinguished itself by replicative studies. IRG III represents the third refinement in the endeavour to describe student involvement in both educational and sporting settings.

Box 4.1 - Students'behaviours: Studies and Papers reviewed

Aufderheide (1980)	(Auf80)
Aufderheide,McKenzie & Knowles (1982)	(A,M,K82)
Brunelle,Godbout & coll. (1980)	(B,G,80)
Cheffers,Brunelle & Von Kelsch (1980)	(C,B,K80)
Cheffers & Wuest (1983)	*(C&W83)
Costello (1977)	(Cos77)
Costello & Laubach (1978)	(C&L78)
De Paepe (1985)	(DeP85)

Dodds (1983a)	(Dod83a)
Godbout,Brunelle,Tousignant (1983)	(G,B,T83)
Griffin (1980)	(Gri80)
Griffin (1983)	(Gri83)
Griffin (1984)	(Gri84)
Griffin (1985)	(Gri85)
Laubach (1975)	(Lau75)
Laubach (1983)	*(Lau83)
Lucas & Read (1982)	(L&R82)
Mancini, Wuest, Clark & Ridosh (1983)	(Man83)
Martinek & Karper (1982)	(M&K82)
McLeish,Howe & Jackson (1981)	(M,H,J81)
Metzler (1979)	(Met79)
Metzler (1983b)	*(Met83b)
Paré,Lirette & Caron (1983)	(P,L,C83)
Piéron (1982a)	(Pie82a)
Piéron (1982b)	(Pie82b)
Piéron & Cloes (1981)	(P&C81)
Piéron & Dohogne (1980)	(P&D80)
Piéron & Forceille (1983)	(P&F83)
Piéron & Haan (1980)	(P&H80)
Piéron & Haan (1981)	(P&H81)
Placek & Randall (1986)	(P&R86)
Rate (1980)	(Rat80)
Rife, Shute & Dodds (1985)	(R,S,D85)
Shute, et al. (1982)	(Shu82)
Siedentop,Tousignant & Parker (1982)	*(S,T,P82)
Telama,Paukku,Varstala,Paananen (1982)	(Tel82)
Telama et al. (1985)	(Tel85)
Telama et al (1986)	(Tel86)
Tousignant (1982)	(Tou82)
Varstala,Telama & Akkanen (1981)	(V,T&A81)

* Papers dealing only with the description of instruments

Box 4.2 - STUDENT BEHAVIORS: Instruments of observation & Methods
      of gathering data

INSTRUMENTS:

(C,B,K,80)   Individual Reaction Gestalt (IRG II)
               6 Obs
               Outdoor activities
               Study of reliability

(Lau,75)   Behavior of S in Physical Education (BESTPED)
               Construct & content validity, reliability

FIELDS STUDIES:

(Auf,80)   60 regular, ALT-PE
(A,M,K,82)   14 T, 120 S (60 mainstreamed handicaped,
               Users vs non users of individualized instruction

(B,G,80)   60 T, elem (30), second (30), live, ALT
               Various subject matters
               School level, subject matter, class size,
               equipment

(Cos,77)   193 S, elem, T, videotape, BESTPED
(C,L,78)   Various subject matters
               Student gender, class size, grade level,
               class segment

(Cro,77)   96 S, 3 Cl, JHS, Good and Brophy Interaction
               analysis system
               Comparison of low and high achievers

(DeP,85)   30 S mentally retarded, ALT-PE (M)
               3 treatment groups: peer environment,
               self-contained environment, specific
               mainstreamed environment.

(Dod,83)   1 T, 17 S, 8 less, ALT-PE (1979 version)
             Tharp - Gallimore obs intrument
             Lacrosse
             Descriptive, correlational

(G,B,T,83)   Same data as (B,G,80)
             Comparison according to school level

(Gri,83)   3 T, 6-7th grades, 20 Less
             Qualitative student participation, S-S IA
             Gymnastics

(Gri,84)   2 T, 6-8th grades, Coed., 34 Less, F. St.
             Qualitative, student participation
             Team sports

(Gri,85)   3 T, 6-8th grades, Coed., 55 Less, M. St.
             Qualitative, student participation
             Team sports

(L&R,82)   20 Cl, JHS, video, BESTPED, STOL (System of
             teaching observation by Lucas)
             Various subject matter

(Man,83)   30 T, 60 Cl, video, CAFIAS, ALT-PE
             Maslach Burnout Inventory (MBI)
             Comparison of 10 randomly Teachers selected in
             low-burnout and high burn-out groups

(M&K,82)   3 T (1M, 2W), 128 S, elem, Dyadic CAFIAS
             Gymnastics and games
             Expectation, motor ability, T & S behaviors

(M,H,J,81)   104 Less, video, ALT-PE
             Various subject matters
             Process - process

(Met,79)   (92 S, 32 Cl, 21 T, live, ALT-PE
             Various subject matter
             Grade level

(Pie,82a)   156 S, 13 Cl, second, live, OBEL,ULg
Gymnastics, volley ball
School level, subject matter

(Pie,82b)   224 S, 56 Cl, ST, second, live, OBEL/ILg
Volley ball, gymnastics
Comparison of low and high achievers

(P&C,81)   132 S, 13 T, 10 ST, 23 Cl, second., video
OBEL/ULg
Gymnastics, volley ball
Teaching experience, school level, subject matter

(P&F,83)   192 S, JHS, OBEL/ULg
Volleyball, gymnastics
Comparison of high and low achievers

(P&H,80)   300 S, JHS, T, live, OBEL/ULg
(P&H,81)   Team sports, Track and field, gymnastics
Subject matter, gender & coed.

(P,L,C,83)   7 T, 21 Adap Cl, 42 Less, ALT-PE
Comparison according to different types of Cl
(grouping according to the handicapped
characteristics)

(P&O,80)   292 S, SHS, ST, live, OBEL/ULg
Gymnastics, volleyball
Gender, subject matter

(P&R,86)   20 T (7 specialists - 13 non specialists), élém -
ALT-PE (II)
ALT-PE (II) variables
Comparison between sp. and non-specialists

(R,S,D,85)   2 T, 36 & 18 ST, videotapes, ALT-PE I, II
Volleyball, badminton
Comparison of the two versions of ALT-PE

(Rat,80)   46 Cl, ALT-PE
Various subject matter mainly Basket ball

(Shu,82)	105 S, 20 Cl, 1 T, live, ALT-PE Comparison of low, medium and high achievers
(Tel,82)	524 S, 263 Less, 77 T, elem, second, vocational, live Gender, objectives
(Tel,85)	812 S, 406 Less motor engagement and intensity of participation according to the subject matter taught
(Tel,86)	802 S, 406 Less student behavior according to sex and to leisure activities ("sport club activists", "recreational sport activists", "passive"
(Tou,82)	3 T, 127 Less, ethnographic technique Qualitative study
(V,T,A,81)	20 Cl. Indoor activities, 3 Swimming Cl. Process - process (T behaviors - S behaviors)

TIME TO LEARN: THE "FUNNELING EFFECT".

An important concept has emerged from observing student engagement time (time spent on task). It must be considered at different levels:

(1) Allocated time for physical education: that is the time allocated by school authorities to physical activities. In many countries it ranges from 1 to 3 hours per week.

(2) Functional time: physical education teachers are not able to use all the allocated time. Students loose a part of it to come to the gym or to the sports field. Minutes are devoted to dressing or to administrative duties. It will be necessary to remove something from the amount of time allocated to the physical education program before finding a real measure of the time spent on the sports field. After observing 52 teachers, Zakrajsek

(1974) found out that approximately one third of the allocated time for physical education was used to dress, for roll call, shower ....

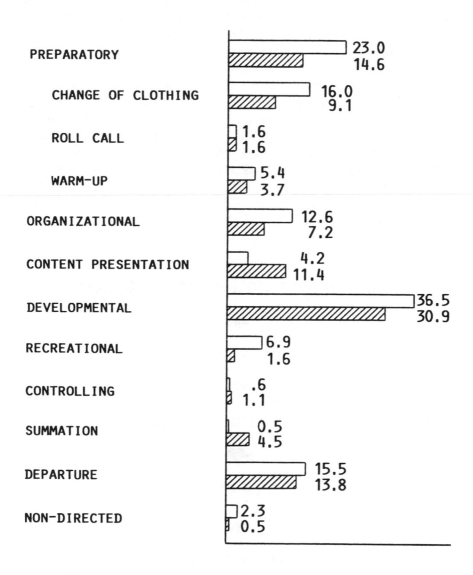

Figure 4.1 - Instructional Time Utilization (Zakrajsek, 1974).

(3) Allocated time for practice: once on the field, teachers organize their classes, motivate students and present activities. Students have to prepare material and equipment. A new subtraction must be made before finding how much time students can devote to practice. If teachers talk a lot, if they spent too much time in management, the allocated time for practice will be further reduced.

(4) Motor engagement time: That is the key notion: the time spent by students in practising physical activities. It is easily understood that a student cannot remain active during the whole period allocated to practice. Equipment often limits participation and recovery periods are urgently needed after maximum efforts. However aimless long waiting periods considerably effect the amount of engaged time. Metzler (1979, 1982) used the term "funneling effect" to describe the series of subtractions to be made from the allocated time for physical education.

ALLOCATED TIME TO PHYSICAL EDUCATION

FUNCTIONAL TIME

ALLOCATED TIME TO PRACTICE

MOTOR ENGAGEMENT TIME

TIME-ON-TASK

Figure 4.2 – Student engagement time: the funneling effect.

Student Behavior

Several variables around the concept of motor engagement
time according to learning opportunities received attention.

Several Experimental Teaching Units (ETU) underscored that
the motor engagement time variable has to be stated more accurately before gaining a full predictive value of teacher effectiveness in physical education. The specificity of the tasks prac-
tised and the level of success achieved in performing the task
must be taken into account. Significant learning occurs only when
some prerequisite level of performance is fulfilled (Piéron
1982c, 1983b). The difficulty of the task (is it a proxy for
success rate?) is included in the ALT-PE instrument.

Most of the field studies are articulated around the comparison of student'behavior profiles according to context variables
(gender, grade or school level, class size, lesson format, number
of students per class) and programme variables (subject matter
taught, methodology of teaching, objectives).

PROFILE OF STUDENTS BEHAVIOR.

One striking observation is that a subject matter whose
objective is movement is mostly characterized by non movement
periods. Results from BESTPED or OBEL/ULg (Costello & Laubach,
1978; Piéron & Cloes, 1981) studies were largely confirmed by ALT
studies (Godbout, Brunelle & Tousignant, 1983).

Thirty percent of the time devoted to movement activities is
frequently the upper limit of the data reported by several authors (Costello & Laubach, 1978; Piéron & Haan, 1981). Data
gathered in ALT studies reported lower percentages. Costello &
Laubach (1978), Piéron & Haan (1980), Piéron & Dohogne (1980) and
McLeish, Howe & Jackson (1981) reported data ranging between 20
and 30 % for engaged time or ALT-(PE)M. Brunelle et al. (1980),
Metzler (1979), Shute et al. (1982) reported data lower than 20 %
and sometimes in various groups of students, lower than 10 %.
Another series of data has to be underlined: 34 % of ALT in an
observation of interscholastic sports groups or classes (Rate,
1980). An interesting exception is reported by Varstala, Telama &
Akkanen (1981): 46 % of time spent in movement observed in indoor
lessons. In this percentage, 20 % were classified as intense

activity. These data were confirmed by Telama et al. (1982) with 46 % and 52.1 % of pupils'activity, in girls and boys.

The variability of figures reported is extremely high from class to class. Examples are easy to find: movement time ranged from 13.1 to 69.2 % of the time in the classes observed by Costello and Laubach (1978). Other examples can be taken from the same study for subcategories such as: game playing (0 to 56.1 %), practice (from 0 to 47.5 %), exercise (from 0 to 20.2 %). The same kind of observation has been made in the McLeish, Howe & Jackson study (1981): the task - practice - motor - easy category varied from 0 to 60 % and averaging at 25 %.

The figures come generally from a melting pot of different kinds of lessons. Subject matters are frequently quite different. Except the paucity of movement conclusion, very little other can be drawn from these data.

CONTEXT VARIABLES.

An important variable could be cultural differences and expectations across the range of this considerable international research agenda.

STUDENT GENDER. Telama et al. (1982) observed a significant difference between boys and girls in motor engagement time (52.1 - 46.0 %, p < .01). In the other studies reviewed, differences were generally small but in four out of five studies, boys were more frequently engaged in motor activities (boys: Costello & Laubach, 1978; Piéron & Haan, 1980, Shute, Dodds, Placek, Rife & Silverman, 1982; Telama et al., 1982; girls: Piéron & Dohogne, 1980).

SCHOOL AND GRADE LEVEL (Tab. 4.5). Up to now, data reported are contradictory and seem to be inconclusive. Junior high school students were reported to be more active than senior high school students (Metzler, 1979; Piéron, 1982a). In the Costello and Laubach study (1978), upper grade students spent more time in game playing and in practice than lower grade students. Brunelle et al. (1980) observed that elementary school pupils and secondary school pupils were motor engaged for approximately the same percentage of time (19.7 - 19.3).

Table 4.5 - Student motor engagement.

Variable	Data	School level	Authors
GYMNASTICS			
MET	16.7 %	Senior H.S.	Piéron & Dohogne (1980)
MET	18.3 %	Senior H.S.	Piéron & Forceille (1983)
ALT-PE	21.9 %	Junior H.S.	Rate (1980)
MET	22.3 %	Junior H.S.	Piéron & Haan (1981)
MET	21.3 %	Junior H.S.	Piéron & Cloes (1981)
MET	22.1 %	Elementary	McLeish, Howe & Jackson (1981)
BASKETBALL			
ALT-PE	35.9 %	Junior H.S.	Rate (1980)
MET	51.0 %	Junior H.S.	Piéron & Haan (1980)
VOLLEYBALL			
MET	28.8 %	Junior H.S.	Piéron & Dohogne (1980)
MET	25.9 %	Elementary	McLeish, Howe & Jackson (1981)
VARIOUS			
MET	30.0 %	Elem. & H.S.	Costello & Laubach (1978)
ALT-PE	19.7 %	Elementary	Brunelle et al. (1980)

When differences occurred between younger and older students, they were explained by the fact that frequently younger students practice easier activities with the class acting as a whole. Frequently they seemed to be more interested in physical activities that older students.

CLASS SIZE. Data from the Costello & Laubach study (1978) did not confirm that class with fewer numbers of students were more involved in physical activity than larger sized classes.

PROGRAMME VARIABLES.

SUBJECT MATTER TAUGHT (Tab. 4.5). The subject matter taught seems to be one of the strongest variables affecting the time spent in motor engagement by the pupils in physical education classes. Team sports are frequently located at the upper level of students engagement (McLeish, Howe & Jackson, 1981; Piéron et Haan, 1980; Piéron & Dohogne, 1980; Rate, 1980). Swimming also involves a high level of students activity (McLeish, Howe & Jackson, 1981). Gymnastics is frequently found at the bottom of the activity ranking (McLeish, Howe & Jackson, 1981; Piéron & Haan, 1980; Piéron, 1982a; Rate, 1980). Five gymnastic lessons observed by Costello & Laubach (1978) out of twenty overall lessons observed were ranked amongst the six less active lessons.

It must not be concluded that superiority of one subject over another or discreditation of the educational value of acti-vities should stem from lessons involving less motor engagement time. An all-out effort like an athletic jump or a basket ball "lay-up" can hardly be compared. These differences imply that the teacher must deal with different problems when students are involved in physical activities during most of their allocated time than when non active periods are predominant. In gymnastics, for instance, it could be better to use a variable like the number of trials performed instead of the motor engagement time variable.

TEACHING OBJECTIVES. With the subject matter variable, tea-ching objectives are amongst the most potent variables affecting the pupils' motor engagement time. Telama et al. (1982) observed that motor engagement time amounted to 54 % of the observation time in lessons where fitness objectives were set forth. The motor engagement time was lower with recreational objectives (47 %) and with motor skill learning objectives (45 %). Differen-ces between fitness objectives and the other objectives were significant at .05 and .01 levels. These data were also supported by results from questionnaire inquiries dealing with the pupils' assessment of the physical strain of the various types of physical education lessons.

Table 4.6 – Student behavior according to main objective of physical education lesson (Telama et al., 1982).

	Main Objective			
	(1)	(2)	(3)	(4)
	Recreation	Fitness	Learning	Other
1. Organizing	9	10	9	9
2. Waiting for organization	12	9	10	9 1-4*
3. Following teaching of subject matter	6	8	12	11 1-3*** 2-3**
4. Following other guidance	1	1	1	1
5. Getting feedback	2	2	2	2
6. Carrying out task (time-on-task)	47	54	45	50 1-2* 2-3**
7. Waiting for turn	19	9	16	14 1-2*** 2-3**
8. Helping somebody else	0	1	1	0 2-4*
9. Other activities arising from observation	1	1	0	0
10. Other activities	1	1	0	0
	100 %	100 %	100 %	100 %
N =	86	108	144	177

CLASS SEGMENT. Students spent the largest portion of their practice time in the middle of the class. They also spent the largest part of their game playing in the latter part of the class (Costello, 1977; Costello & Laubach, 1978).

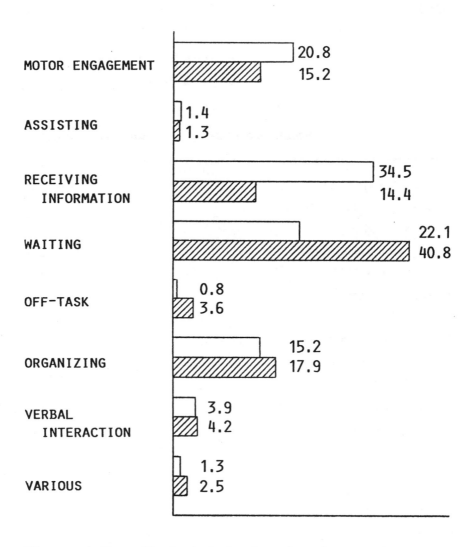

MOTOR ENGAGEMENT 20.8 / 15.2

ASSISTING 1.4 / 1.3

RECEIVING INFORMATION 34.5 / 14.4

WAITING 22.1 / 40.8

OFF-TASK 0.8 / 3.6

ORGANIZING 15.2 / 17.9

VERBAL INTERACTION 3.9 / 4.2

VARIOUS 1.3 / 2.5

Figure 4.3 - Student behavior in classes taught by master teachers [ ] and by student teachers ▨

Engaged time in motor activities was smaller during learning periods than for the overall lesson time. In learning periods, students are mostly involved in group activities. Material and equipment frequently limit student participation.

TEACHING EXPERIENCE.

The student engaged time was strikingly higher in classes managed by master teachers than in classes managed by beginners (Piéron & Cloes, 1981; Piéron & Georis, 1983). Master teachers were defined according to several criteria: length of teaching experience, ratings by supervisors, role of model played in in-service training courses (Piéron, 1982a). The difference can probably be attributed to two factors: (1) maintaining a close contact with pupils by frequent interventions dealing with content (task presentation and feedback); (2) a better management enabling master teachers to transform the allocated time for practice in more pupil motor engagement time than the beginners or student teachers can do.

LOW AND HIGH ACHIEVERS.

A few studies compared the engagement time of low and high achieving students (or of exceptional students) being mainstreamed. Shute et al. (1982) observed relatively small differences in the "motor easy engaged" category between high achievers (16 %), low achievers (13 %) and medium achievers (11 %). The differences were higher between special needs students (6 %) and "normal students" (18 %).

Piéron (1982b) observed 224 low and high achievers in gymnastics and in volleyball classes. In the two settings, low and high achievers differed significantly. The differences were strikingly higher when specific motor skill learning activities were concerned. He concluded that when considering the motor engagement time and success rate variables, high achievers found more opportunities to learn than low achievers. When examining the student engagement and the level of success of the activities performed, it could be concluded that the gap between high and low achievers could be expected to widen. These results have been confirmed by Piéron & Forceille, 1983 (Figure 4.4).

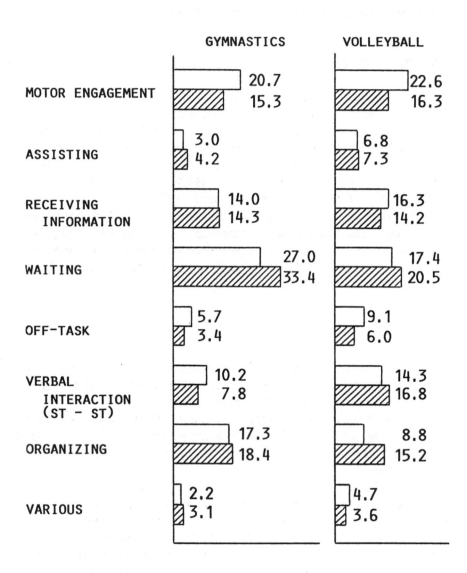

Figure 4.4 - Behavior of high achievers ☐ and of low achievers ▨ in gymnastics and volleyball classes.

QUALITY OF PARTICIPATION.

Systematic qualitative observation of teaching physical education is rather uncommon. In that kind of observation, no preexisting system is used. The categories are developed inductively from the description of occuring events.

Recently, Tousignant (1982) observed 127 class periods during a long span of time (5 to 10 weeks). The narrative accounts of the event happening in the classes included descriptions of the various elements of the task structures: (1) the demands made on the students; (2) the context surrounding the task accomplishment; (3) the accountability system or the contingencies operating in the classes; (4) the teacher actions to initiate and enact the task accomplishment; (5) the students' responses to the demands of the tasks; (6) the patterns of task development.

Four basic categories of students behaviors were extracted from the data: students engaged in the task as stated by the teacher, students engaged in a modified task, students engaged in deviant behaviors, students avoiding participation without misbehavior (bystander).

The students appeared to behave according to what they were held accountable for. They seemed to gather the information concerning the "real task requirements" from the teacher's reaction as well as the absence of reaction (Tousignant, 1982).

Girls' and boys' participation styles were identified through the use of qualitative observation, informal interviews with the teachers and a formal interview at the end of the study (Griffin, 1984).

In girls, participation patterns were observed during 34 team sport class observations over an 8 week period. Six styles were identified: "Athletes" (high visibility and involvement, included by boys in the game interactions, assertive in their interactions with boys), "JV Players" (average or low skilled, enjoyed the game and expressed excitement about playing), "Cheerleaders" (vicarious involvement, low skilled players, seemed to accept their status), "Lost souls" (invisible noninvolvement, low skilled, appeared to panick at the prospect of handling the ball), "Femmes fatales" (blatant non involvement, very concerned about their physical appearance), "System beaters" (usually absent from physical education classes).

Griffin (1984) described four kind of nonassertive behavior characteristic of the majority of the girls observed: (1) giving up, (2) giving away, (3) hanging back, and (4) acquiescing.

In boys, fifty-five team sport classes were observed, and three physical educators were interviewed about their perceptions of student participation. Five styles of participation were identified: "Machos" (highly skilled and enthusiastic about team sports, verbally agressive with other pupils, and frequently initiating interaction with the teacher), "Junior Machos" (similar to the machos in their participation, tending to be physically smaller than the machos, less skilled, and sometimes more resentful of skilled girls than machos were), "Nice Guys" (sometimes as skilled as the machos and frequently more skilled than the junior machos, generally more accepting in their interaction with girls and other boys), "Invisible players" (experts at appearing to be involved in games without really participating), "wimps" (low-skilled in team sports, teased by machos, junior machos and even by some girls) (Griffin, 1985).

Qualitative data could provide a useful image of students and/or teachers behaviors and supplement quantitative data provided by the actual systems of observation.

DISENGAGED TIME.

Disengaged time, a counterpart of motor engagement time, seems to be negatively related to teacher effectiveness. Several behaviors considered not productive as far as learning objectives are concerned were observed to last for a large amount of class time, sometimes exceeding 35 % of that time. Disengaged time must be considered in a broader sense simply, waiting time. It could be viewed as unproductive time for the teaching and learning processes. Besides waiting periods, interim periods and off task periods can be added. It is defined as a time during which students are resting, waiting their turn to practice, waiting for the teacher to begin an activity (Costello & Laubach, 1978;

Piéron & Haan, 1981; Piéron & Dohogne, 1980). Telama et al. (1982) make the interesting distinction in waiting time as that occuring during organization of the class or during teaching periods.

These periods frequently represent a larger part of the lesson time than the engagement time. They can amount to more than a third of the observation time. They occur during the observation periods labeled content general in ALT studies. They are defined as periods of no activity or no movement between activities. They are generally short and represent less than 5 % of the time. They are the most important part of the categories labeled content physical education. Distinction is made between waiting, off task or interim, this category dealing with the behaviors during the management of the class.

Comparisons are hard to make between different authors according the gross size of these waiting periods. It must be noted that Rate (1980) observed disengaged periods of 40.2 % of the observation time. Shute et al., 1981; Costello & Laubach, 1978; Metzler, 1979) observed not engagement periods ranging from 30 to 40 %. Students observed by Piéron & Haan (1980) and by Piéron & Dohogne (1980) were shown to be disengaged during from 20 to 30 % of their time. Telama et al. (1982) observed the smallest amount of disengaged time, less than 20 %. European Education appears to tolerate shorter periods of disengaged time than U.S. Education.

The practical implication of high amounts of disengaged time is that opportunities to learn are definitively lost. Piéron (1982a) observed that the disengaged time was significantly related to the occurence of off task behaviors.

Authors have focused less on sources of variation of this variable. Students are generally more frequently active in high school or in higher grade levels, from elementary to senior high school level (Metzler, 1979; Piéron & Cloes, 1981). Girls were observed to be disengaged more frequently than boys by Costello & Laubach (1978). This result was confirmed by observation from the same authors in coeducational classes. Piéron & Haan (1980) observed an opposite tendency to have boys less active than girls.

Data comparing different subject matters must be looked at very carefully for a practical point of view. Differences observed by Piéron & Haan (1980) must be thought over: disengaged time in team sports, 15.7 %, in gymnastics, 33.45 and in track and field, 46.6 %.

Within team sports and dual sports specialities, data from McLeish, Howe & Jackson (1981) do not identify a clear tendency. The lower value observed was in badminton (16.1 %), the higher in tennis (26.5 %), 17.8 % in volleyball and 22.6 % in soccer.

Comparison of data according to class size provided some unexpected data: the wait time was higher in small classes (less than students) than in large classes (more than students) (Costello & Laubach, 1978).

INTERACTION WITH THE TEACHER.

When observing target students the interaction image is quite different than data provided by interaction analysis based mainly on the teacher. From 55 to 80 % of events can be classified as non interactive events (Piéron & Cloes, 1982). Interactive events are of two types: (1) interactions of active - passive character when the teacher is talking, mostly solliciting and the student (as part of a group or of the entire class) is silently listening, and (2) a dyadic interaction when target pupil and teacher are talking together or when the teacher is providing the student with kinesthetic cues or with feedback. This individual interaction amounts approximately to 1-2 % of all events recorded for the student.

The dyadic interactive events occuring in a class must be looked at very carefully. Many teachers behaviors included in the interactive events, like augmented feedback and praise, are considered as enthusiastic behaviors by students in physical education teaching (Caruso, 1980). More striking is the fact that many non interactive events are clearly designated as unenthusiastic behaviors, and considered as disinterest, withdrawal from the group, or detachment (Caruso, 1980).

Student Behavior

In classroom teaching several experiences showed that some differences in behaviors could be expected from teachers in their interactions with students according to their perceptions of student skills. Good & Brophy (1978) reported minor differences in the frequency of teacher contacts with pupils of different achievement levels. They found more important variations in the quality of these contacts.

CHAPTER 5

RESEARCH ON TEACHER EFFECTIVENESS

EXPERIMENTAL TEACHING UNITS

Chapter written by Maurice PIERON & George GRAHAM
(Virginia Polytechnic Institute and State University,
Blacksburg, Virginia)
Updated from a publication in the
International Journal of Physical Education

THE MODEL.

During the last decade, teacher accountability and teacher effectiveness have received significant amounts of attention. The question "What does make a difference between more and less effective teachers ?" has been asked with increasing frequency. The art of teaching is influenced by so many factors, however, that the answer to this question cannot be answered by identifying a single variable or even a limited series of variables. Successful teaching involves the orchestration of a complex set of variables and only a few of these variables have been identified consistently through teaching research.

In classroom teaching research, the process-product paradigm has contributed to the identification of several variables found to be frequently related to student learning gains (Berliner & Tikunoff, 1976; Rosenshine, 1980). Teacher behavior and student behavior (what is happening in the class) has been studied in relation to what was learned by the students. These behaviors, identified by systematically observing the teaching process, converge towards the concepts of increased opportunities to learn for the students, often termed "student engagement" or "teacher monitoring".

In physical education full scale process-product studies employing the same design as the classroom studies, can hardly be envisaged. Studies of the magnitude of the classroom teacher effectiveness research require resources not usually allocated to research in teaching physical education. One alternative to the full scale process-product research paradigm has been Experimental Teaching Units (ETU) or ETU like experiences. The ETU provides a small scale process-product setting enabling one to make reasonable guesses about important variables related to teacher effectiveness. According to Graham (1983), an experimental teaching unit (ETU) is a brief series of lessons on a topic that is of general interest to the grade level of students to be taught by the teachers in the experiment. The ETU model mandates a controlled setting (sometimes a micro-setting) in which the content to be taught is standardized. In ETU studies, the learning environment is reduced in terms of time, space, number of students. ETU are characterized by:

1. A measure of student learning developed specifically to measure the instructional content taught in the ETU which is administered before and after the actual ETU lesson(s) are taught;

2. An universal learning objective set forth for all the teachers;

3. A relatively short teaching period;

4. Systematic observation of selected teacher and student behaviors conducted during the actual ETU lesson(s).

Thus far, only a few ETU studies have been completed in physical education. Although there are variations in design, it is possible to review them according to their main components: tasks to be learned by students (the content of the ETU), length of the teaching period(s), student and teacher characteristics and the size of the class taught.

Box 5.1 - Teaching Effectiveness: Studies and papers reviewed

---

Brunelle et al. (1985)	(Bru85)
Carlisle (1981)	(Car81)
De Knop (1983a)	(DeK83a)
De Knop (1983b)	(DeK83b)
De Knop (1985)	(DeK85)
Graham, Soares & Harrington (1983)	(G,S,H,83)
Metzler (1983a)	(Met83a)
Paese (1986)	(Pae86)
Phillips & Carlisle (1983b)	(P&C83b)
Piéron & Piron (1981)	(P&P81)
Piéron (1982c)	(Pie82c)
Piéron (1983b)	(Pie83b)
Salter & Graham (1985)	(S&G85)
Silverman (1983)	(Sil83
Silverman (1985a)	(Sil85a)
Silverman (1985b)	(Sil85b)
Yerg (1977)	(Yer77)
Yerg (1981a)	(Yer81a)
Yerg (1981b)	(Yer81b)
Yerg (1983)	(Yer83)
Yerg & Twardy (1982)	(Y&T82)

Box 5.2 - Teaching effectiveness (studies based on ETU) -
        Design of studies

(Bru,85)   37 Pl, 20 Less, ALT-PE
                  Ice Hockey (evaluation of specific motor skills)
                  Achievement scores and variables related with
                  ALT-PE system

(DeK,83a)   8T (6M, 2W), 15 hours teaching per T
(DeK,83b)   Tennis: backhand, forehand, service
(DeK,85)   Variables: measures of learning, T evaluation,
                  T behavior, S behavior, motor fitness and
                  ability, S knowledge, motivation
                  Process - Product

(G,S,H,83)   11 T, elem, average Cl size: 27
                  Task: novel motor skill (hockey)
                  Variables: presage, time on task, instruction
                  activity, instruction management, management,
                  waiting, different kinds of feedback

(Met,83a)   2 ST, 77 S, elem, 7 groups
                  Task: same as (G,S,H,83)
                  Variables: from ALT-PE (M)

(Pae,86)   10 ST (2 groups), 20-26 S/Class, 20 min Less,
                  ALT-PE
                  Task: novel motor skill, same as (G,S,H,83)
                  Variables: from ALT-PE

(P&C,83b)   18 T, 144 S, elem & second, PETAI
(Car,81)   Volleyball: 10 lessons
                  Variables: Analyzing S needs, T instruction time,
                  T management time, S allocated skill learning
                  time, S management time, S achievement

(P&P,81)	10 T, 40 S, univ, video, OBEL/ULG
(Pie,82c)	Task: handstand roll over (gymnastics)
	Variables: time on task, time spent in practicing the criterion task, number of trials augmented feedback
(Pie,83b)	1 T, 16 S, SHS, OBEL/ULg, 5 Cl periods (35 min)
	Task: roundoff to backhand spring (gymnastics)
	Variables: Time on task, Task specificity, success rate, augmented feedback
(S&G,85)	4 ST, 244 S, gr 3 to 6, 20 min
	Novel golf task
	Teaching styles: command, guided discovery, no instruction
	Variables: motor skill performance, skill attempts, cognitive learning, student's rating of self efficacy.
(Sil,83)	45 S, 17 to 31 Y, ALT mod
(Sil,85a)	Task: breaststroke (arm action, leg action, body
(Sil,85b)	position, breathing, and coordination
	Variables: motor engagement, cognitive engagement, managerial activities, waiting, off-task
(Yer,77)	40 T, 120 S, elem, video, TBOS
(Yer,81a)	Task: cartwheel (gymnastics)
(Yer,81b)	Variables: Feedback, Task presentation, opportunity to practice
	Comparison according to: T cartwheel performance, T knowledge, learner cartwheels performed, T demonstration
(Y&T,82)	32 T (11 M, 21 F), 128 S, elem, 15 min., TBOS
	Task: balance beam (gymnastics)
	Variables: S ability level, practice composite, task presentation, feedback

---

DESIGN CHARACTERISTICS.

TASKS. Different kinds of tasks have been selected from the sports of gymnastics, tennis, volleyball, swimming and golf. The following tasks were taught as ETU content in the reviewed studies: the cartwheel (Yerg, 1977, 1981a, 1981b), the handstand roll over (Piéron & Piron, 1981; Piéron, 1982c), the handstand round off and back handspring (Piéron, 1983b), and balance beam exercise (Yerg & Twardy, 1982), a novel golf swing (Graham, Soares & Harrington, 1983; Metzler, 1983a; Salter & Graham, 1985), the forehand, the backhand and the service in tennis (De Knop, 1983a), the breaststroke in swimming (Silverman, 1983, 1985a, 1985b), and volleyball skills, (Phillips & Carlisle, 1983b).

ETU LENGTH. The length of the unit and the number of lessons is a function of the relative ease or difficulty of learning a task. For this reason, there are rather extreme variations in the length of the ETUs. The total teaching time of the ETU lessons varied from a single 15 minute lesson in the Yerg and Twardy study (1982) to 15 hours of instruction over a series of lessons in the study of tennis teachers by De Knop (1983).

STUDENT AND TEACHER CHARACTERISTICS. Teachers, as well as students involved in the studies, differed strikingly, from undergraduate pre-service teachers (Piéron, 1982c; Yerg, 1977) to experienced teachers (De Knop, 1983; Graham, Soares & Harrington, 1983; Piéron, 1983b), from elementary school students (Graham et al., 1983; Salter & Graham, 1985; Yerg, 1977; Yerg & Twardy, 1982) to physical education university freshmen majoring in physical education (De Knop, 1983b; Piéron, 1982c).

CLASS SIZE. Classes varied from micro-setting size (3 students) in the Yerg's study (1977) to full class size (average of 27 students) in the studies by Graham, Soares & Harrington (1983) and Salter & Graham (1985).

OVERVIEW OF COMPLETED STUDIES.

DESIGN. Although the design of the physical education ETU studies varies within the parameters of the ETU paradigm, the first Yerg study (1977) provides a representative example.   In her study, achievement in the cartwheel was the criterion mea- sure.   The independent variables selected for their assumed im- pact on student performance were: teacher knowledge of content, task presentation by the teacher, teacher guidance and support of practice, teacher provision of specific task related feedback (figure 5.1).   Forty pre-service physical education teachers taught a twenty minute lesson to three randomly assigned students from grades three through six.   Pre-test and post-test student performance and the teacher performance were filmed.   Teacher behaviors were observed through the Teacher Behavior Observation System (TBOS).   Multiple regression was used to determine rela- tionships between final performance as a function of pupil ini- tial performance and the teacher behavior variables.

In a more recent study, Yerg and Twardy (1982) employed a paradigm similar to Yerg's first study (1977).   In this study, a task on the balance beam served as dependent variable.

Piéron & Piron (1981) and Piéron (1982c) also used a gymnas- tics skill, the handstand roll over, in an ETU study to compare more effective and less effective teachers based on the learning gains of their students.

Graham, Soares and Harrington (1983) determined the diffe- rences in employement of selected variables by more effective and less effective in-service teachers when teaching a novel motor skill to entire classes of elementary school children.   The ETU task was similar to a golf stroke. Children struck a rubber ball using a plastic hockey stick into a hoop target.

The same ETU design was also used to study the influence of three different teaching approaches-- command, guided discovery and no-instruction (Salter & Graham, 1985). In this study expe- rienced teachers taught different classes of children, but same the teachers taught lessons using both the command and guided discovery approach.

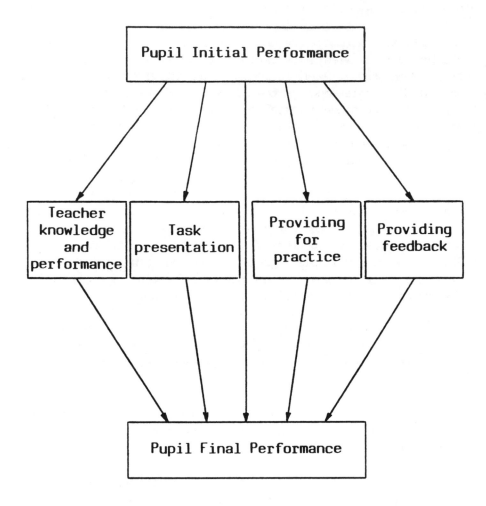

Figure 5.1 - Model of Classroom process (Yerg, 1981a)

Metzler (1983a) used the same task as Graham et al. (1983), in a ETU lesson taught by two graduate students to children. In this study, two strategies, "lecture demonstration" and "reverse chaining" served as independent variables. In addition, the length of time allocated for the ETU lesson varied between 20, 30 and 40 minutes. Academic Learning Time - Physical Education was used to systematically analyze the ETU lessons. A control group that received no teacher instruction was also allocated 20 minutes for practice of the novel task.

The main purpose of the other study by Piéron (1983b) was to focus on the students in a real class and to compare students learning more and students learning less in the same teaching conditions. This study departs slightly from other studies in that the focus was on individual students, and their learning gains. The teaching unit lasted longer than in most of the other studies, five 35 minute class periods, except the De Knop (1983b) and the Phillips and Carlisle (1983b) studies. The teacher was let free to select the skill to be learned by the students. He decided to teach the gymnastic routine "roundoff to back handspring".

The study by De Knop (1983b) is certainly one of the best conceived studies among the ETU physical education paradigms. Eight tennis teachers taught a 15 hour teaching unit to future physical education teachers. Two additional groups practiced under trial and error conditions without the presence of any teacher. Special care was devoted to the analysis of students gains in the areas of skill improvement, technique and motivation.

Phillips and Carlisle (1983b) measured teacher effectiveness during a ten lesson beginning volleyball unit. Student achievement on five volleyball skill tests served as the dependent variables. The amount of time teachers and students were engaged in selected variables, measured by the Physical Education Teaching Assessment Instrument (PETAI), comprised the independent variable (Phillips & Carlisle, 1983a). PETAI consists of three teacher and three student behavior categories (analyzing student needs, teacher instruction time, teacher management time, student allocated skill learningtime, student management time, and student achievement) and their subcategories.

Silverman's study (1985a, 1985b) could explain the presence or absence of the relationship between student engagement and student outcome. He investigated the relationship among student achievement, student engagement, and selected student characteristics of initial skill, previous experience, and sex in an ETU based on teaching the breaststroke to students ranging from 17 to 31 years of age. Instruction consisted of four 15 minute classes.

FINDINGS.

Findings of the ETU studies can be discussed as several topics including: improvement of student performance, influence of student skill entry level, role of student engagement time and success, task presentation, and teacher feedback.

IMPROVEMENT OF LEARNER PERFORMANCE. Fortunately all the studies showed some improvement of learners performance. Three of the studies, De Knop (1983b), Metzler (1983a) and Salter & Graham (1985) used control groups who practiced the criterion task but without teacher instruction. The studies reported conflicting outcomes. In De Knop's study, the learning gains of the students in the trial and error groups were less than in the groups performing under the direction of the teachers. In Metzler's study, however, the control group that practice the task for 20 minutes on their own had learning gains that were virtually identical to the group that received 20 minutes of instruction. This finding was replicated in the study by Salter & Graham (1985). They were able to explain this outcome because the students in the No-Instruction Group had significantly more skill practice attempts than students in either the Command or Guided Discovery Groups.

INFLUENCE OF ENTRY LEVEL. Entry level appears to be one of the most important variables in studies of short term duration. Yerg (1977, 1981a) observed that 75 % of the total variance of the final level of achievement in the task was explained by the entry level of performance. Two percent was explained by teacher's intervention, and 23 % remained unexplained.

The variance was lower in other studies: 46 % in the Piéron & Piron study (1981) and 31 % in the Yerg and Twardy study (1982). De Knop (1983b) found that the amount of entry level skill explained by the final performance varied according to different aspects of the performance: 17 % for the skill test, 18 % for motivation and 56 % for the technique. The lower values skill and motivation could be due to the relatively long teaching period (15 hours) as compared with the relative brevity of the other ETU studies.

STUDENT ENGAGEMENT TIME. Most of the studies corroborated the importance of the time spent practicing the criterion task or the number of practice trials. Students who learned more had teachers who provided them with more time to practice the criterion skill.

It is important to emphasize, however, that the measure of time on task was not identical for each of the studies. The measures were related and included as process measures in most of the studies.

Time allocated for practice, as compared with time students actually spend practicing, was found to be related to teacher effectiveness only in the study on tennis teachers (De Knop, 1983b). Metzler (1983a), Piéron & Piron (1981), Phillips & Carlisle (1983b) used the same variable without finding any significant differences on the amount of time allocated by more effective and less effective teachers in physical education. Metzler's findings suggest that improved performance in the ETU was not a direct function of increased allocated time for students. Just being in class longer does not guarantee greater achievement.

Actual time on task, also referred to as engagement time and Academic Learning Time (although the latter also uses a measure of task difficulty), is a measure of actual student involvement during allocated time and is therefore a more stringent measure of what students actually do during a lesson. In an additional analysis of her 1977 study data, Yerg (1981a) found a positive relationship between the amount of practice and achievement scores. She stressed the importance of building a meaningful composite score to evidence particular differences. Additional analyses by Yerg of the same data indicated that teacher behaviors that interfere with practice were negatively related to student achievement.

This observation seems to be confirmed by a similar observation in Piéron & Piron's study (1981). In a comparison of micro-classes distributed according to average gains students achieving more learning gains tended to practice more than those who didn't improve as much.

Phillips and Carlisle (1983b) also found that engaged skill learning time was a distinguishing factor related to teacher effectiveness. In fact, they reported that teachers in the more effective group provided their students with more than twice the amount of engaged skill learning time than did the less effective teachers in their study.

Several studies provide data converging in the same direction although without statistical significance (Graham et al., 1983; Yerg, 1977). In the Yerg study (1977), the practice component appeared to be positively influencing the learners outcome. Its influence was greater than the teacher knowledge of the cartwheel, for example, or the teacher ability to perform the cartwheel. In contrast, the practice component was negatively influencing the pupils'outcome in the Yerg and Twardy study (1982). In their discussion, they indicated that in this study the allocation of practice time may have been a "default option" because the teachers in the ETU did not have the background to know what feedback to provide and therefore they simply remained passive observers once the learners achieved a certain degree of competence.

Student success when practicing the criterion tasks was also observed in several studies. A higher success rate in specific students was evidenced in the high learning group when compared with the low learning group (Piéron, 1983b). Success during engaged skill learning was also found more often in the classes of more effective teachers in the study by Phillips and Carlisle (1983b).

In the ETU on swimming, when all students were analyzed together, no engagement variable correlated significantly with residualized achievement. When the three skill levels were analyzed using a separate regression equation (Silverman, 1985a, 1985b), engaged time was significantly correlated with achievement for highty skilled students. On the contrary, for moderately skilled students engaged time was negatively correlated with residualized achievement. The question of the mediating effect of the characteristics of the subsample studied on the relationship between student achievement and engagement rates must still be clarified.

In this instance, the physical education data are in agreement with data from the classroom research. The role of time on task was emphasized in a number of classroom studies and related positively with student learning in reading and in elementary math (Berliner, 1979; Berliner & Tikunoff, 1976).

TASK PRESENTATION. The clarity of a teachers presentation along with the amount of time teachers spent actually instructing a class were variables considered in several studies. Essentially the finding was that there is no clear relationship between either the clarity or conciseness of a teachers instruction and student learning.

Yerg (1977) reported that only 2 % of the total variance of the final level of achievement were explained by teachers variables. One of these variables in her study was the clarity of the teacher's presentation.

Although Graham et al. (1983), and Phillips and Carlisle (1983b) did not measure the clarity of instruction they did analyze the amount of time teachers spent in instruction. Both studies found that the amount of instruction time failed to distinguish between more effective and less effective teachers in physical education.

Future research efforts in this area probably need to focus more on the variables closely related to the quality of the teachers presentation, rather than on simple measures of time. Variables such as clarity, appropriate instruction and use of demonstration, may lead to a better understanding of the function of a teacher's instruction in enhancing student learning.

TEACHER FEEDBACK. Divergent results were reported concerning the relationships between teacher feedback and learning outcomes in ETU studies. Reworking her previous results, Yerg (1980) observed that on one hand, feedback to a single student referring to the total movement was positively related to pupil achievement and on the other hand, detailed informative feedback was negatively related to pupil outcome on the same criterion. Graham et al. (1983) did not find any significant difference between the amount or type of feedback used by more effective and less effective teachers.

Several studies showed a facilitating role for teacher feed-back. Students practicing in the more effective microclasses received a higher proportion of augmented feedback (Piéron, 1982c) although it must be remembered that students in these classes also spent a higher proportion of time in actual practice. In learning a beginning balance skill, teacher feedback was found to positively influence student learning (Yerg & Twardy, 1982). The positive feedback was higher for more effective teachers in the volleyball unit (Phillips & Carlisle, 1983b). One interesting finding emerged from the study on tennis teachers, feedback accounted for 11 to 16 % of the total variance of final level in accuracy or skill and technique measures (De Knop, 1983b).

IMPLICATIONS.

The significance of this series of physical education ETU studies resides in the obvious fact that many of the findings are corroborative. The research designs and the independent and dependent variables in the studies reviewed were related, not identical, and yet they have produced confirmatory results.

The strongest finding of these studies supports the class-room finding (Berliner & Tikunoff, 1976; Rosenshine, 1980) that students of more effective teachers spend more of their time on task, actually practicing appropriate skills, than students in less effective teachers classes. In fact, this result is so universal in both the research on classroom teachers, and now on physical education teachers (De Knop, 1983b; Metzler, 1983a; Phillips & Carlisle, 1983b; Piéron, 1982c; Piéron & Piron, 1981; Yerg, 1977, 1981a) that is has begun to appear as an axiom in discussion of effective teachers. It is probably as close to a research supported universal truth as there is in the study of teaching.

Obviously, however, the findings related to teacher perfor-mance, in classes that have high on-task time by students, are far from axiomatic. We know that students in more effective teachers classes practice appropriately more often but a descrip-tion of the teachers'actual performance in these classes has yet to be corroborated through research. In fact, three of the studies in this review (De Knop, 1983b; Metzler, 1983a; Salter and Graham, 1985) included classes that had no teacher instruction and yet all reported learning. Two of the Three approached that of a group that received instruction by a teacher (Metzler, 1983a; Salter & Graham, 1985).

Task presentation and teacher feedback are the two teacher behaviors that have been included most frequently as independent variables in the physical education ETU studies (Graham et al., 1983; Piéron, 1982c, 1983b; Phillips & Carlisle, 1983b; Yerg, 1977; Yerg & Twardy, 1982). Neither a teachers clarity nor the time spent instructing an entire class has yet to coalesce as an indicator of physical education teacher effectiveness (Graham et al., 1983; Phillips & Carlisle, 1983b; Yerg, 1977). Teacher feedback, however, shows promise as an indicant of teacher effectiveness (De Knop, 1983b; Phillips & Carlisle, 1983b; Piéron, 1982c, 1983b; Yerg & Twardy, 1982) although care must be taken to equate student time on task if it is to be studied effectively as an independent variable.

The series of physical education ETU studies that have been completed thus far have only provided a glimpse into the orchestration of skills that comprise successful teaching. The research based glimpse, however, is better that the conflicting and virtually opaque mosaic of conventional wisdom that dominated notions about "good" teaching prior to the 1970's. Additional ETU studies in physical education have the potential to provide an even more informed answer to the question "What does make a difference between more effective and less effective teachers of physical education?".

CHAPTER 6

THE COACH

Observation Instruments
Descriptive studies
Verification of methodologies used in coaching
Teaching and coaching situations
Coaches behavior modification

It could be asked if it is really necessary to develop a chapter dealing with coach behaviors in a book centered on the study of the teaching process. In many instances, the coach does not pursue educational aims. However the coach must transmit knowledge to the players, create a supportive climate and help the players to achieve learning outcomes.

Coaches act in a communication situation and exert their action through verbal and non verbal interventions. Usually their aims are more accurately defined than teachers and more consistent to their players aims than with the students aims.

Without dealing here with the role conflict problem, it must be considered that the same people may undertake both roles: teacher and coach.

To study coach behaviors and interventions, it is considered frequently that observers have used the same instruments or those closely related to observation schedules used in teaching. Specific instruments must abide to the same rules of reliability and validity with those used in teaching.

OBSERVATION INSTRUMENTS.

(a) Originating from the study of teaching.

Mancini & Agnew (1978) report the results of an unpublished study in which physical education classes and sport activity classes were observed by means of CAFIAS, an instrument currently used in physical education research.

Bain (1976a, 1976b, 1983b) developed an instrument to identify the implicit values of physical education curricula. It can be used in sport settings. Darst, Mancini & Zakrajzek (1983) categorized it into the schedules for coach observation.

(b) Specifically developed to study coaching behaviors.

(1) The observation schedule of Tharp & Gallimore (1976) has been mainly used in case studies focusing on top level coaches, namely John Wooden, the famous UCLA basketball coach, a basketball coach and a football coach observed by Lucas (1980) and another football coach analyzed by Langsdorf (1979).

(2) The Coaching Behavior Assessment System (CBAS) developed par Smith, Smoll & Hunt (1977). Coaches behaviors are dealt with in two major groups of categories: reactive behaviors and spontaneous behaviors. Reactive behaviors are responses to identifiable stimuli immediately after player's behavior (desirable performance, mistakes or errors, and misbehaviors); the other group of categories are spontaneous behaviors, initiated by the coach and not a response to an immediately preceeding event (game

related or game irrelevant). The observation schedule has been used in descriptive studies or studies linking the overt behavior to the perceived behaviors, and in behavior modification through a teaching programme. It has been slightly modified by Brunelle et al. (1980) to observe teachers.

(3) LoCoBAS, Lombardo Coaching Behavior Analysis System (Lombardo, Faraone & Pothier, 1982). It is a five category instrument centered around the concept of evaluation: positive, neutral and negative and around task related (on-task) or task irrelevant (off-task) behaviors.

(4) a more original approach is that of Brunelle et al. (1978a, 1978b). As a first step in their study, the authors have developed a theoretical concept and a model based upon teaching methods and training techniques. Secondly, they have determined observable behaviors corresponding to these principles before building their observation schedule. Brunelle et al. (1978a, 1978b) have studied ice hockey coaches and instructors.

(5) Rushall (1975a) developed two observation schedules, which are easy to use and focused on the coach and on the athlete. They can be adapted to be applied in studying the teaching.

(6) The "Systematic Coaching Observation by Lucas" (S.C.O.L.) (1980) is very close to the Tharp & Gallimore observation system.

Box 6.1 - Coaches behaviors: Studies reviewed

Bain (1978)	(Bai78)
Bain (1983)	*(Bai83)
Brunelle et al.(1976)	(Bru76)
Brunelle et al.(1978a)	(Bru78a)
Brunelle et al.(1978b)	(Bru78b)
Fisher et al. (1982)	(Fis82)
Gonçalves & Piéron (1986)	(G&P86)
Hould & Brunelle (1981)	(H&B81)
Kasson (1974)	(Kas74)

Lacy & Darst (1984)   *(L&D8)
Langsdorff (1979)   (Lan79)
Langsdorf (1983)   *(Lan83)
Lombardo, Faraone & Pothier (1982)   (Lom82)
Lucas (1980)   (Luc80)
McKenzie (1986)   (McK86)
McKenzie & Rushall (1980)   (M&R80)
Quarterman (1983)   *(Qua83)
Rushall (1975)   (Rus75)
Rushall (1983)   *(Rus83)
Rushall & Smith (1979)   (R&S79)
Smith, Smoll & Hunt (1977)   (S,S,H,77)
Smith, Smoll & Curtiss (1979)   (S,S,C,79)
Smoll, Smith, Curtiss & Hunt (1978)   (Smo78)
Spallanzani, Brunelle, Trempe (1981)   (S,B,T,81)
Tharp & Gallimore (1976)   (T&G76)
Wuest et al. (1986)   (Wue86)

* Papers dealing only with the description of instruments.

Box 6.2 - Coaches behaviors: Instruments & methods of gathering
          data

INSTRUMENT:

(S,S,H,77)   5 & 21 obs, Coaching Behavior Assessment
               System (CBAS), video
               Description & reliability

FIELD STUDIES:

(Bai,78)   20 T (10 M, 10 W, 20 C, IVI-PE
               Various subject matters
               Gender, situation (teaching - coaching)

(Bru,76)	48 C, specific instrument, audio
(Bru,78a)	ice hockey
(Bru,78b)	Descriptive data: source of intervention, direction, mode
(Fis,82)	50 Teams (C - Pl), CAFIAS, Group Environment Scale Basketball Satisfied vs Less satisfied team climates
(G&P,86)	6 M (C & T) OBEL/ULg - FEED/ULg Basketball Teaching vs Coaching settings
(H&B,81)	12 C, 45 sessions, 6 Pl? session, ALT-PE Ice hockey Organization forms
(Kas,74)	3 M, IA teaching vs coaching verbal/non verbal
(L&D,85)	10 C, High School, Tharp & Gallimore mod. Football Preseason, early season, late season
(Lan,79)	1 C, Tharp & Gallimore Instrument Football Descriptive
(Lom,82)	34 C, Lombardo Coaching Behaviour Analysis Various subject matter Descriptive
(Luc,80)	2 C, Tharp & Gallimore Instrument, SCOL Basketball, Football Descriptive
(McK,86)	3 Pl, ALT-PE mod Volleyball (top level athletes) Descriptive

(M&R,80)	2 C, 32 S (16 boys, 16 girls), swimming Behavior modification Experimental conditions: Provision of positive and negative statements, Behaviour game Variables: inappropriate behaviour (changing stroke, stopping, not swimming in, not pushing off)
(Rus,75)	? C, DCOS & DAOS Ice hockey, basketball, volleyball, swimming, Football
(R&S,79)	1 C, Coach Observation Schedule Swimming Behaviour modification
(S,S,C,78)	51 C, 542 Pl, CBAS Player perception and attitude, observed and player- perceived behaviors, observe, perceived and player attitude
(Smo,78)	34 C, 10-15 y level, CBAS Coaching skills: training to relate more effectively with children Exp (n=18), Cont (n=13)
(S,B,T,81)	60 C, 3 age groups (n=20), CBAS Ice hockey
(T&G,76)	1 coach (outstanding) Basket ball Descriptive
(Wue,86)	1 C (F), 12 Pl (F), 18 sessions ALT-PE, version II Volleyball Comparison of High-, Average-, and Low-skilled athletes

DESCRIPTIVE STUDIES.

A case study, on John Wooden is probably the best known study of the relationship between a coach and his athletes. It was completed by Tharp & Gallimore (1976). For basketball fans, it seems to be unnecessary to present largely John Wooden, coach of the UCLA basketball team during more than a decade. He won approximately ten university championships with his UCLA team in approximately 15 years.

In deciding to observe an exceptionally successful coach, Tharp & Gallimore approached the basic questions: How does an exceptional coach behave? How does an exceptional teacher teach? How does teach a teacher able to achieve his aims and objectives teach so well?

Tharp & Gallimore (1976) observed systematically John Wooden during fifteen training sessions during the same season. They have registered a total of 2326 teaching acts (Table 6.1).

The observation system has been tested several times on teachers. It was modified to include two interventions particular to John Wooden, one labeled "Scold - reinstruction", ie. a critique or reprimand immediately followed by an indication of how to perform well. The other intervention was hustling.

Table 6.1 - John Wooden (Tharp & Gallimore, 1976)

Instruction	50.3 %
Hustle	12.7
Positive Model	2.8
Negative Model	1.6
Praise	6.9
Scold	6.6
Non Verbal reward	1.2
Non Verbal punishment	Trace
Scold - Reinstruct	8.0
Othe	2.4
Uncodable	6.6

These results prompt several comments. Wooden devoted a large part of its interventions to instruction (50.3 %). He emphasized what has to be done and how to do it. In the observation system, no category was provided for the organization events. It can be thought that several interventions dealing with the organization of the team well included in these 50.3 % categorized as instruction. However other interventions clearly showed that the "How to do" is predominant (model - reinstruction), in the teaching approach of Wooden.

Disapprobatory instructions were almost always followed by an indication of coach expectations. They induced a reinstruction or the presentation of a positive model.

A special concern was given to the "hustles" aiming at intensifying players efforts and involvement. This kind of behavior amounted to 12.7 % of teaching interventions. When the 6.9 % praises and 1.2 % non verbal reward were added to the hustles, it can be infered that the coach established some supportive climate (although 6.6 % are scolds). Such a picture was largely different from data gathered in teaching. The category "hustle" was seen as uncessary or rarely used in teaching observation schedules.

Another study has been completed using the same observation instrument by Lucas (1980) with two Canadian head coaches in basket-ball and football. Six practice sessions (mid season and late season practices) were observed on a random basis. Two systems of observation were used, the Tharp & Gallimore (1976) and the system for coaching observation by Lucas (S.C.O.L.). like John Wooden, the coaches observed in this study placed a strong emphasis on the instruction category (44 to 58 % of the verbal comments by the coach). This study also pointed out the importance of categories such as "Hustle" (20.6 % in the basketball coach and 18.7 % in the football coach), to praising the athlete (19.3 and 13.5 %) and the reinstruction after scolding the player (6.0 and 4.5 %). Several similarities were observed between behaviors observed in these two coaches and John Wooden.

Smoll, Smith, Curtiss & Hunt (1978) observed 51 male coaches and 542 players by means of the CBAS in baseball games. Players experience ranged from 8 to 15 years.

Table 6.2- Mean CBAS (Observed) and Player-Perceived scores for each behavior category (Smoll, Smith, Curtiss, & Hunt, 1978).

Behavior Category	Observed[a]	Player-Perceived[b]
Reinforcement	17.1	5.3
Nonreinforcement	4.2	2.7
Mistake-Contingent Encouragement	3.1	5.2
Mistake-Contingent Technical Instruction	4.2	5.3
Punishment	1.8	2.5
Punitive Technical Instruction	1.0	2.7
Ignoring Mistakes	3.7	2.9
Keeping Control	1.7	5.4
General Technical Instruction	27.3	5.3
General Encouragement	21.4	5.7
Organization	8.4	5.6
General Communication	6.1	4.7

a The values represent the percentage of behaviors falling into each category.

b The values represent the mean score on a 7-point scale reflecting frequency of occurence of each behavior

The authors observed that approximately two-thirds of the behaviors fell in three categories: reinforcement, general technical instruction, and general instruction. Punitive behaviors were low when compared to other behaviors. An interesting point in the discussion of the results of this study must be carefully thought by teachers as well as by coaches:

"Although there are areas of correspondance between observed and perceived behaviors, the factor analytic data indicate that the pattern of overt behaviors is different from the organization of perceived behaviors. The different factor structure underlying perceived behaviors may reflect the additional influence of cognitive and attitudinal factors on the interpretation and the organization of a player's perception of his coach." (Smol, Smith, Curtiss & Hunt, 1978).

VERIFICATION OF METHODOLOGIES USED IN COACHING.

A study is a good illustration of this research approach. It has been completed on ice hockey coaches by Brunelle et al. (1978b). The authors aims were to describe teaching strategies used by coaches. The authors tried to answer three questions:

1. Do ice hockey instructors respect general teaching principles issued according to teaching and learning principles?

2. Do ice hockey instructors apply instructions dealing with the right way to teach?

3. Do they use strategies unknown or unused by physical education teachers?

Two kinds of teaching principles have been selected: those related to the climate (sociological, psychological and affective aspects: not to hurt or blame participants, maintain friendly relationships, husstle or stimulate the participants activity) and those dealing with the organization of learning conditions (presenting, explaining, and organizing task without to much talking, giving feedback to participants, individualizing instruction.

Forty eight instructors has been observed in a natural coaching setting. The observation pointed out that instructors:

(1) used teaching acts dealing with organization of the lesson three times more often than with the content;

(2) emphasized husstle for completion more than praise for efforts already accomplished;

(3) used four times the interventions to correct errors or mistakes than to put some emphasis on the success achieved by the athletes;

(4) used four times more praise than scolds and that they provided twice as much feedback (related to content) than to intervene on affective aspects of the coach - athlete relationship.

TEACHING AND COACHING SITUATIONS.

An important question is to know whether the same individual does behave the same way with a class or with a group of athletes.

In Kasson'study (1974) behavior of three physical education teachers at the university level and of the same people involved in sports activities were videotaped in wrestling, baseball and gymnastics. The observation schedule was a slightly modified version of the system used by Mancuso (1972, 1983).

The conclusions of the study were as follows: the analysis of direct and indirect behaviors showed a significant difference in favor of direct behaviors observed more frequently in the teaching situation than in the coaching situation. Verbal behaviors were observed to be used more frequently in teaching than in coaching. In the teaching situation, indirect verbal behaviors were more frequent than indirect non verbal behaviors. In the coaching situation, indirect non verbal behaviors were dominant.

In a paper refering to an unpublished study, Mancini and Agnew (1978) reported that they observed 20 female teachers (secondary school level) by means of the CAFIAS during teaching and sport training sessions. In coaching, the teacher - student interaction was more visible; more pupil behaviors were teacher initiated and praise and encouragement were more frequent in teaching than in coaching. The interaction was seen as more flexible in the sports group than in the class.

In a more recent study, Gonçalves & Piéron (1986) have used different observation instruments focusing alternatively on coach/teacher augmented feedback and on athlete/student behavior. Six males teachers have been observed six times: three times in a class setting and three times during coaching practice sessions in basketball. All teachers were experienced both in teaching and in coaching basketball.

Clear differences were observed in the educational settings students and young athletes were engaged in. Use of reduced game situations were more frequently in the coaching setting than in the school setting (19.2 % vs 4.6 % of the time spent in the gym). This difference was balanced by a larger proportion of time spent in the full game situation (20.9 % vs 14.9 %) and in devoting a larger part of the time in providing information to the participants (28.0 % vs 23.0 %) in teaching than in coaching. Time spent in practicing "drills" was very close in teaching and in coaching (40.0 % vs 39.8 %). Motor activities not directly related to the basketball tasks were more frequent in teaching (6.0 %) than in coaching (3.0 %).

The percentage distribution of activities selected to be practiced by players and students showed that the full game participation was higher in teaching. The game-like situations were more frequent in coaching. Student involvement and opportunities to learn within these two settings differ. In game-like situations (2 x 2, 3 x 3) ...), players have more opportunities to be directly involved in the main actions and to be in contact with the ball, a unique source of progress for beginners. Moreover scrimmage or game-like situations have been shown to facilitate the motor engagement of the participant and to reduce the number of failure in taking part in the game.

More advanced participants can derive probably more benefit from taking part in the full game competition. These differences seem to be in contradiction with the quality of the participants. Athletes might benefit more from the competition than students.

The choice to give such a prominent place to a full game setting with students could not be explained by the higher number of participants in the class than in the sport team. Usually this situation leaves many players outside the court, more than with a more structured class organization. The concern to keep them "busy and happy" in choosing a less demanding and more attracting situation was a possible explanation.

The direct motor engagement of the participants was significantly higher (T = 0, P = .05) in coaching (37.2 %) than in teaching (24.8 %). Differences in favour of the coaching situation was observed as well for the category "player in contact with the ball" as when the player was taking part in an action closely related to the ball.

The indirect engagement is limited to a mere presence on the field during a full game competition, without being close to the action. No difference was observed in teaching and in coaching (7.7 - 7.6 %).

Waiting periods (30.1 % - 23.2 %) and cognitive engagement (28.4 % - 23.0 %) were higher in teaching than in coaching.

The feedback intervention rate amounted to 2.5 per minute (one intervention every 24 seconds) in coaching and 2.4 in teaching. The rates did not differ significantly in the teaching and coaching situations.

Rate of feedback was in the range of rate reported in the literature, slightly higher than those reported for teachers (Arena, 1979; Fishman & Tobey, 1978) but lower than in teachers involved in their special area of expertise (Brunelle & de Carufel, 1982; Piéron & Delmelle, 1981).

Slight differences were observed in the feedback functions. There was a tendency to use more frequently evaluative and prescriptive feedback in coaching than in teaching. On the contrary, descriptive and interrogative feedback were more frequent in teaching than in coaching.

More striking differences were identified when dealing with more accurate specific feedback functions: in the coaching situation, approbative feedback and positive prescriptive feedback were used more frequently than in the coaching situation. In the teaching setting, negative prescriptions were more frequent. Negative affective feedback were more frequent in teaching than in coaching.

It has been suggested that coaches rely almost exclusively upon direct style of communication with players (Lombardo, Faraone & Pothier, 1982; Sherman & Hassan, 1986; Smoll, Smith & Curtiss, 1978). The data gathered in this study about feedback confirm this trend of coaches to use a direct approach. Prescriptive feedback was the more frequent category observed and it was largerly higher in coaching than in teaching. The reason for directness related probably to the nature of the objectives set forth by the coach to the players. Direct instruction is considered to be effective in academic classroom teaching (Rosenshine, 1978). When the objectives are clear, as it is in coaching, Flanders hypothesized than the direct approach must be used. The emphasis on direct instruction may not set problems in the group climate. It is probably warmer and friendlier in coaching than in teaching due to a large amount of approbatory evaluative feedback and to positive prescriptive feedback.

Teachers tended to induce more reflexion by asking more questions in guiding students to discover their errors or by giving a larger amount of descriptive feedback.

Several factors converge to indicate that players were provided with more opportunities to learn than students. Moreover they seem to make a more frequent use of these opportunities with a higher motor engagement.

COACHES BEHAVIOR MODIFICATION.

Smith, Smoll & Curtiss (1979) developed a preseason training program purposing to improve the relationship between the coach and his/her players. Observation has been made during baseball training session. The behavioral guidelines were derived from a preliminary investigation. They were based on the relationships between observed coach behaviors, players' perceptions and recall of such behaviors, and players attitudes.

The training programme used several techniques: oral and written presentation of the guidelines, "modeling", feedback and self-analysis. In the intervention programme, the techniques were designed.

> "To make coaches more aware of their behaviors, to create
> expectancies concerning the likely consequences of various
> coaching behaviors, to increase their desire to generate
> certain consequences rather than others, and to develop or
> to enhance their ability to perform desirable effectively.
> It was expected that cognitive changes of this nature would
> promote and mediate positive changes in overt coaching beha-
> viors". (Smith, Smoll & Curtiss, 1979).

Eighteen coaches were randomly assigned to the experimental
group and 16 coaches to the control group. In general, the guidelines stressed the desirability to use reinforcement, praising,
encouragement, and technical instruction. The stated goals of the
programme were to increase positive interaction between coach and
players, as well as among teammates, and to reduce fear of failure among players.

Coaching behaviors were assessed by means of the CBAS (see
above). The use of reinforcement interventions was the major
discriminator between the two groups, higher in the experimental
group than in the control group. It was the behavior most highly
emphasized in the training program.

Experimental group coaches were perceived as more frequently
engaged in reinforcement, mistake contingent encouragement, and
general technical instruction, and as less frequently in non
reinforcement, punishment, and punitive technical instruction.
These differences were consistent with the programme objectives
and the behavioral guidelines (Figure 6.2).

We have referred to another technique for changing the
teacher behavior. It consists in the application of a determined
program on a unique subject following a multiple baseline. This
kind of study can be found also with coaches.

The study by Rushall & Smith (1979) focused on changing the
quality and the quantity of interventions of a swimming coach.
Results corresponded to the expected change: frequency of rein-
forcements and of feedback increased after the intervention.
Apparently, the verbal repertoire of a coach can be largely

augmented by this kind of intervention programme.

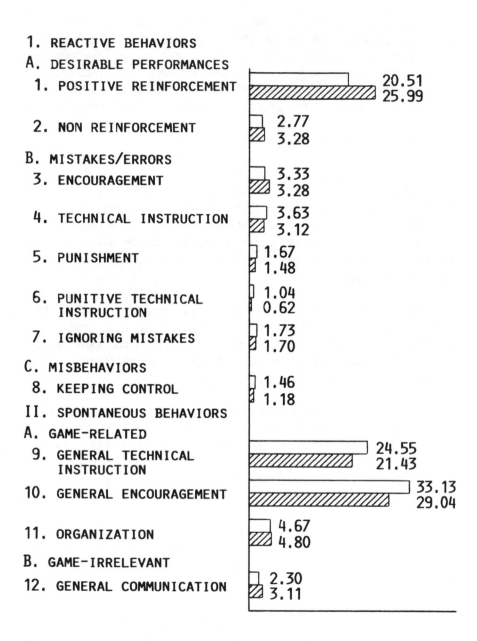

Figure 6.1 - Observed behaviors (CBAS) of experimental and control group coaches (from Smith, Smoll, & Curtiss, 1979).

Mertler (1974) investigated the degree to which coaching behavior can be modified and whether the changes in coaching behavior will affect some player behaviors. The subject were a young female basketball coach and four randomly selected team members. The study was divided in two phases, each consisting of a series of interventions on a dual baseline. The first phase consisted of interventions on coach behavior and analysis of any associated change in player behavior. The second phase called for specific interventions on participant behaviors when the changes effected in coach behavior during the first phase failed to show changes in player behaviors.

The coach behavior categories were close to those targeted in teacher behavior modification studies at Ohio State University: managerial events, monitoring, no activity, positive and negative informative feedback, positive reactions to on-task behaviors, negative reactions to off-task behaviors. Five categories of behaviors were observed in participants: length of managerial episodes, amount of participation, level of effort applied when performing a defined task (considered as maximal, adequate, or inadequate), inter-personal reactions, and performance skills (shooting percentage, rebounding, losses of possession of the ball. Before intervention, coach behaviors were primarily negative or corrective reactions. The coach focused on what players were doing wrong. Intervention was effective in changing several coach behaviors to various degree. However, with the exception of active participation, changes in the coach behaviors during the first phase did not produce a modification in players behaviors. The absence of any noticeable effect of coach behavior change upon player behavior was also observed by Rushall (1982).

CHAPTER 7

TEACHER PREPARATION

The analysis of teaching leads naturally to application in pre-service teacher preparation in addition to in-service training. Of real concern for those who are in charge of teacher preparation programs is that of determining good knowledge of what is really happening in a class. Competencies of acquisition and teaching for pre and in-service teachers are highly dependent on this knowledge. Factual information by itself is insufficient to change teaching behavior. Direct involvement in the teaching - learning process appears to more readily bring about change.

Locke & Dodds (1984) stated that: "Research on teacher education (ROTE) refers to research with deals with any aspect of the process designed to influence what teachers will do in the execution of professional tasks. Put another way, ROTE is re-search on teaching teachers how to teach. Most of the research reviewed in this section of the text deals with the process variables, i.e. the delivery of professional skills. Another part is concerned with the preparation for specific skills, as defined by Locke & Dodds categories.

As in the other sections of our text, research reported will be based on observation. However, other research instruments like the critical incident technique, although not specifically obser-vation based, provides some insight in the teaching process during student teaching (Schempp, 1985) or on the interaction between the cooperating teacher and the student teacher (Brunelle, Tousignant & Piéron, 1981; Piéron, Brunelle & Tousignant, 1981).

QUESTIONS AROUND TEACHER PREPARATION.

Systematic observation of teaching aims at identifying and at describing the characteristics of teaching styles, of teaching patterns, of teaching events, and to estimate their impact on the student achievement. One can easily understand that many ques-tions emerge from an accurate description of the teaching pro-cess, especially when teaching the teacher:

* Is it possible to learn teaching skills, teaching strate-gies, and teaching styles?

* Once learned, is it possible to maintain the level of expertise gained through the intervention program and keep some reasonable optimism to improve them?

* How can we change behaviors stereotyped by years of rou-tine teaching?

For too long, teacher preparation programs in colleges of education have used different means to facilitate the first contact between the future teacher and the sometimes tough rea-lity of a real class. Examples such as peer teaching, student teaching, and internship come to mind. Student teaching has been considered and is still considered to be the most useful teaching preparation experience. However, its impact has not always been substantiated by research. For example, teaching patterns as described by the observation through the "Verbal Interaction Category System - VICS) did not change during a eight week student teaching experiences (Mawson, 1973) and serious questions have been raised about field-based experiences (Zeichner, 1980).

"Most criticism of present practice center around the argument that field-based experiences are conservative institutions which serve merely to socialize prospective teachers into established patterns of school practice" (Zeichner, 1980).

Most of these techniques have been systematically included in teacher preparation programs without any systematic research analysis of their real impact on student teachers.

* Are these techniques able to help the student acquire and master specific teaching skills?

* Are teaching skills practiced in adapted, simplified and to some extent artificial conditions transferable to more demanding classroom or gym settings?

* Is it possible to transfer teaching skills mastered within the framework of a specific subject matter or from one grade level towards another?

Many other questions must be raised.

Two approaches were usually considered to study systematically the impact of different techniques or procedures devised to master teaching skills and improve the teacher-student relationship:

(1) a training program, frequently in interaction analysis as a means to change the global teacher-student interaction;

(2) the use of specific interventions in view to change some specific teacher or/and student behaviors.

In some instances, specific intervention using the behavior modification approach and comparison of treatment and control groups were combined.

The common domain of study was as follows: teacher-student interaction, acquisition and modification of teacher behaviors, modification of student motor engagement, and working out of intervention procedures.

Box 7.1 - Teacher preparation and teacher behavior modification: Studies and papers reviewed.

Birdwell (1980)	(Bir80)
Boehm (1974)	(Boe74)
Borys (1983)	(Bor83)
Brockmeyer (1976)	(Bro76)
Carlisle & Phillips (1984)	(C&P84)
Cramer (1977)	(Cra77)
Currens (1977)	(Cur77)
Darst (1974)	(Dar74)
Darst (1976)	(Dar76)
Dessecker (1975)	(Des75)
Dodds (1975)	(Dod75)
Dodds (1979)	(Dod79)
Dodds (1983)	*(Dod83)
Ewens (1981)	(Ewe81)
Gaudet (1982)	(Gau82)
Graham (1973)	(Gra73)
Gusthart (1983)	(Gus83)
Gusthart & Rink (1983)	(S&R83)
Hamilton (1974)	(Ham74)
Hanke (1981)	(Han81)
Hughley (1973)	(Hug73)
Hutslar (1976)	(Hut76)
Keilty (1975)	(Kei75)
Mancini, Frye & Quinn (1982)	(M,F,Q,82)
Mancuso (1972)	(Man72)
Mawson (1973)	(Maw73)
McKenzie (1976)	(McK76)

McKenzie (1981)	(McK81)
Reese (1983)	(Ree83)
Rife (1973)	(Rif73)
Rolider (1979)	(Rol79)
Rushall (1975)	(Rus75)
Rushall (1976)	(Rus76)
Rushall & McEachern (1977)	(R&M77)
Saunders (1981)	(Sau81)
Van der Mars, Mancini & Frye (1981)	(M,M,F,81)

---

* Paper dealing only with the description of an instrument

Box 7.2 - Teacher Preparation: Instruments of observation & Method of gathering data.

(Bir,80)   3 T, elem, JHS, SHS, ALT-PE
             Multiple baseline design
             Target behaviors: ALT-PE, ALT-PE(M), Management
             time,, Feedback, Student non engaged time.

(Boe,74)   8 ST, JHS
             Multiple baseline design (CBTE)
             Target behaviors: general positive behavior IAs,
             specific positive IAs, negative behavior IAs,
             general positive feedback, specific positive
             feedback, general negative feedback, first name
             use

(Bor, 83)   8 T (2 M, 6 F), 32 Cl, video, BESTPED
             Exp vs cont.
             Basketball unit
             Target behavior: Motor engagement time

(Bro,76)   6 T, video & audio, Harrington Feedback
             Diversity Classification System
             Target behavior: feedback

(C&P,84)   24 ST, Observation physical education teaching
            assessment instrument, Collins enthusiasm
            rating scale
            Exp vs control groups
            Target behaviors: enthusiasm

(Cra,77)   5 CT, 5 ST
            Multiple baseline design, six week training
            Target behaviors: management instruction, activity
            time, management episodes, positive & negative
            corrective feedback, positive and negative
            behavior statements, appropriate S behaviors,
            active S learning.

(Cur,77)   16 ST, live, placheck, 5 weeks training
            Exp vs Cont groups
            Target behaviors: management time, instruction
            time, activity time, first name use, positive
            general and specific behavioral IAs, negative
            general and specific behavioral IAs, positive
            general and specific feedback, negative general
            and specific feedback.

(Dar,74)   ST (3 M, 4 F), elem, live, T behavior placheck
(Dar,76)   Multiple baseline design (competency based
            package)
            Target behaviors: General positive reactions to
            on-task pupil behavior, negative reactions to off-
            task pupil behavior, general positive instruc-
            tional feedback, specific positive instructional
            feedback, general negative or corrective instruc-
            tional feedback, specific or corrective
            instructional feedback, first name use, direction
            of T feedback
            S Behavior: appropriate / inappropriate; active /
            inactive; time spent in managerial episodes.

(Dod,75)   4 ST, live
(Dod,79)   CBTE, Multiple baseline design
            Target behaviors related to Instructional process
            (7), Instructional feedback (8), Management (3),
            Interpersonal relations (8)

(Ewe,80)   16 ST (7 F, 9 M)
               Exp vs cont groups (goal setting)
               Target behaviors: Feedback, Instruction /
               management time, Use of students'first names.

(Gau82)   5 ST (3 M, 2 F), special needs, video & live,
               Multiple baseline design
               CAFIAS target behaviors

(Gra,73)   20 ST, 4 treatment groups
               Microteaching
               Target behaviors: Feedback, Movement time
               (engagement), Learning by students.

(Gus,83)   20 ST, elem, audiotapes, OSCD-PE
(G&R,83)   Comparison of T behaviors at different levels of
               the field experience.

(Ham,74)   7 ST (4 M, 3 F), T behavior, placheck, live
               CBTE, Multiple baseline design
               Target behaviors: T: different types of feedback,
               managerial episodes
               Student: appropriate / inappropriate, active /
               inactive, time spent in managerial episode

(Han,81)   126 S, HIAS
               Microteaching, 3 groups (Discriminative training,
               Discriminative teaching with additional
               microteaching, control group)
               Target behaviors: Heidelberg Interaction Analysis
               variables

(Hug,73)   2 M, 2 F, elem, live, OSU Teaching rating scale
               Multiple baseline design
               Target behaviors: Input, Managerial intervention,
               monitoring, no activity, Positive and negative
               informative feedback, On-task positive reactions,
               Off-task negative reactions

(Hut,76)   6 ST, elem
              Multiple baseline design
              Target behaviors: Management, Instruction and
              activity time, Management episodes per class, T
              behaviors per management episode, positive,
              negative, specific and general statements, and
              Positive, negative and corrective skill feedback.

(Kei,75)   21 ST
              Exp (n = 11) vs Cont (n = 10) groups
              One semester peer teaching program, 3 weeks
              S teaching program, Instruction in IA
              CAFIAS Target behaviors, T Performance Criteria
              Questionnaire, TSRT, Pupil Opinion
              Questionnaire

(M,M,F,81)   36, (19 M, 17 F), video
              Instruction in IA analysis, CAFIAS,
              T Questionnaire on objectives
              Target behaviors: Perceived vs Observed Behaviors
              (CAFIAS)

(Maw,73)   31 ST, 28 CT, 3 Sup., VICS, TSRT, Questionnaire
              Modification of IA during field experience.

(McK,76)   4 ST, Peer assessment model
              Multiple baseline design

(McK,81)   1 subject, live & video
              Multiple baseline design
              Target behaviors: Rate of using "OK", First name
              use, Positive specific feedback

(Ree,83)   14 ST, elem
              Multiple baseline design
              Exp vs cont groups
              Target behaviors: Rule enforcement, Behavioral and
              skill feedback, Distribution of attention, Use of
              names, Use of class time, Appropriate student
              behavior.

(Rif,73)   2 ST, elem, live
Multiple baseline design
Managerial, Monitoring, No activity, Positive
feedback, Negative feedback, On-task positive
reactions, Off-task negative reactions
S Behavior: appropriate / inappropriate

(Rol,79)   15 ST, 1 T, Teacher enthusiasm
Observational System (TEOS)
Multiple baseline design
Target behaviors selected from TBOS.

(Rus,75)   7 ST, BOSPT Schedule
(Rus,76)   Multiple baseline design
(R&M,77)   Seven replications of an ABA reversal
experimental design
Treatment: Discussion of the observation schedule
and feedback after each observed lesson
Target behaviors: Questionning, Directing,
Explaining, Informing, Managing, Monitoring,
Attending, No activity, Feedback and reward,
Correcting and prohibiting.

(Sau,81)   ST (4 M, 3 F)
Microteaching
Target behaviors: Extended indirect influence,
Extended direct influence, Indirect / direct
ratio, Revised indirect / direct ratio, % T talk,
Extended Student Teacher, Uninterrupted activity,
Extended uninterrupted activity, Individual
Teacher talk, Direct reinforcement of pupil
answers.

MODIFYING TEACHER-STUDENT INTERACTION.

One of the purpose of all types of observation systems is to
provide a reliable picture of teacher and/or students behaviors.
In that way, the teacher receives an informative feedback dealing
with personal educational activities. Several authors have noticed that a teacher is a very isolated professional in great

need of objective feedback. Locke (1979) remarked that the teacher can be psychologically alone in a densely populated area.
Teacher may have little sustained contact with people of their
own kind.

Training in interaction analysis or in teacher observation
has been investigated to verify whether that training contribute
to modify teacher behavior or teacher-student interaction. Studying an observational system is supposed to help the teacher to
become more aware of personal behaviors in the class and of the
availability of a wider range of behaviors, largely wider than
normal.

The design generally used for these studies considers the
following format:

(1) in-service teachers or pre-service teachers are observed
one or several times in determined conditions by means of the
observation system in which they will be trained;

(2) the data gathered through observation serve to form
control and experimental (treatment) groups with limited variance;

(3) the treatment group is prepared to use the observation
system: definition of behaviors to be observed, coding rules,
models of different behaviors, feedback by means of the observation system, and traditional feedback. The control group usually
receives only traditional feedback;

(4) during a second series of observations teachers are
compared on several important representative variables of the
teacher-student interaction. Pre- and post- treatment data are
compared.

The main hypothesis of the Lewis study (1974) was that a
seven week seminar in FIAS would result in desirable changes in
teaching behaviors. Subjects were 25 male health and physical
education student teachers. They were randomly assigned to two
groups. Besides the training in FIAS, the treatment group received FIAS feedback. The results of this study were disappointing in showing that the training did not exert an effect on the

verbal teacher behavior nor on the amount of student talk during classes.

Mancuso (1972) verified the same type of hypothesis: Does training in teaching analysis help the teachers to develop a less direct approach in their teaching than teachers not so trained? Once again, the hypothesis had to be rejected. Moreover, teachers from the treatment group were not found to generate more purposeful motor activity by their students than in the control group.

Keilty (1975) used a better suited instrument for studying the interaction in physical education: CAFIAS. In his study, 11 student teachers were assigned to the experimental group and ten to the control group. The treatment consisted of fifteen hours of instruction in the use and understanding of the CAFIAS before the peer teaching program began. All subjects taught three 8-10 minute lessons during this period; engaged in conferences with their supervisor and peers immediately following each lessons; viewed videotapes of their lessons on the same day, discussed their performance with the investigator and their peers, and participated in the follow-up conference with the investigator to reinforce previous input. During the latter conference, the experimental subjects received additional feedback from the investigator in the form of interpretations of interaction analysis matrices of their lessons.

Very few differences were evidenced between treatment and control groups in the many variables analyzed in the study. However, students perceived student teachers from the treatment group as more indirect and accepting than student teachers from the control group.

The effect of interaction analysis on achieving verbal control of teaching styles in elementary physical education was not confirmed by Lewis (1979). Self-coded feedback from Verbal Interaction Category System - Modified (VICS-M) was no more effective than feedback from a log.

A study was conducted by van der Mars, Mancini & Frye (1981) with the purpose to determine if training was beneficial in changing teacher behaviors and also beneficial for increasing the teachers'awareness of teacher-student interaction. The treatment group received instruction and feedback through CAFIAS in addition to a traditional feedback. Teachers in the treatment group perceived more accurately their behaviors, they were more indirect, and they praised and accepted their students more frequently.

MODIFYING SPECIFIC TEACHING SKILLS.

One of the basic assumptions of teacher training is that teaching skills can be acquired, improved and when improvement has occurred, can be maintained.

Research on behavior analysis generally uses single case experimental designs applying a multiple baseline technique. Rife & Dodds (1978) described some principles of application and underscored the benefits that could be expected. In this kind of research, a small number of accurately defined behaviors are observed and recorded to determine their rate of occurence before any attempt to change them. These measures are used as controls for subsequent comparisons. As soon as the natural rate of events is determined, the investigator applies an experimental intervention to one of the behaviors. The other behaviors are maintained at a baseline level.

Theoretically no change should happen during intervention upon the first target behavior, while its rate should increase under the effect of the intervention variable. The baselines for other target behaviors are used as controls for comparing the effects of intervention on the target behavior. The treatment variable is considered effective when intervention changes the rates of target behaviors while the rates of untreated behaviors remain relatively constant (Rife & Dodds, 1978).

At Ohio State University, Siedentop (1981) developed a programmatic research effort to study behavioral changes of teachers. In physical education activities behavior analysis emphasized a group of strategies inherited from principles of operant psychology.

He described the following major steps in the program: (1) deciding what to change and how to measure it; (2) answering the initial question; (3) toward greater complexity and more reality; (4) developing a systematic format; (5) increasing frequency of observation/feedback while reducing the supervisor's role; (6) self management in student teaching; (7) training the cooperating teacher to be supervisor; (8) add a behavior change project to the student teaching experience (Siedentop, 1981).

Table 7.1 - Target behaviors for modification (Hughley, 1973)

---

1. Input teaching acts
2. Management
3. Monitoring
4. No activity
5. Skill attempt positive informative feedback
6. Skill attempt negative informative feedback
7. Positive reaction to on-task behavior
8. Negative reaction to off-task behavior

The first two steps were dealt with the study of Hughley (1973). The observation categories used to set the baseline of the four students observed during the study and to control the modification in the multiple baseline paradigm used are described in table 7.1. The results showed that:

"1. Directed information feedback is effective in producing teaching behavior changes in physical education student teachers. 2. Beginning teachers in physical education emit primarily negative behaviors. 3. Negative behaviors do not automatically decrease as a result of increases in positive behaviors. 4. The beginning student teacher of physical education is very likely to emit very low rates of feedback either positive or negative. Additional findings indicate that it is most difficult to reward on-task positive behavior and ignore minor disruptions". (Hughley, 1973).

Most of these conclusions were confirmed and complemented in the other studies at Ohio State University. The observation schedule materialized in the OSU Teacher Rating Scale (Hughley, 1983). Interventions to change teacher behavior have been diversified from the basic package, mostly through instructions on the nature of the behavior categories, graphic feedback indicating the behavior events during past class periods, cueing and reinforcement, and goal setting.

The Rife study (1973) was more complex. One important question was asked: does the modification of teacher behavior influence the pupil behavior. Pupils were observed by "placheck" for determining the percentage of pupils engaged in appropriate behavior. Changes in teacher behavior maintained an existing high level of appropriate student behaviors.

Several studies completed under the leardership of Siedentop, were largely influenced by Competency Based Teacher Education principles. Three studies were completed at the elementary level (Darst, 1974), the middle school level (Boehm, 1974) and the high school level (Hamilton, 1974).

In previous studies, it was observed that when a particular behavior was the focus for change, the rate of behaviors usually increased. Nevertheless, when the intervention was removed to focus on an another behavior as prescribed by the research paradigm used, the behavior rate in the previous categories decreased. Two factors came from the main focus of intervention, and the maintenance behavior for observations thereafter (Siedentop, 1981).

With Dodds'study (1975), steps were taken toward the fifth stage described by Siedentop. Dodds developed a peer intervention model in which each peer observed one class per day for the partner. The peer provided immediate feedback to the student teacher. A large number of target behaviors within four verbal teaching behavior modules: instructional process, instructional feedback, management, and interpersonal relations were included in the intervention program. Findings were consistant with previous studies completed in the research program. During the intervention phase, means of 60 out of 68 behaviors changed in the desired direction. No specific maintenance contingencies were organized so 30 of these behaviors fell below baseline during the maintenance phase. Dessecker (1975) worked out a situation allowing student teachers to manage their own behavior change project. During teaching, the student teacher wore a small tape recorder. One class per day was recorded, coded, and analyzed. Data were used for consultation with the university supervisor.

The university supervisor - cooperating teacher - student teacher triad can be a source of negative influence. Frequently the university supervisor argues that the cooperating teacher's puts too strong an emphasis on authority and control. Cooperating teachers usually consider that the university supervisor is too theoretical and removed from the reality of the classroom. Besides economic reasons, it was an important motive why the Ohio program emphasized a shift of role from university supervisor to cooperating teacher in order to make the cooperating teacher the responsible agent, providing all instructions in charge of the goal setting, coding, feedback and other aspects of supervision. Cooperating teachers were trained during workshops. They were given alternatives for managing the student teacher field experience. This approach was successful in terms of reliability of data from observation, magnitude of changes, and maintenance of changes (Hutslar, 1976; Cramer, 1977). For instance, in Hutslar study, the six elementary school physical education student teachers taking part in the program were compared to a similar control group. Significant change in teaching performance occurred for five out of six student teachers in the exprimental group. The regular program did not produced substantial change.

The intervention package used by Ewens (1981) consisted of self-assessment of teacher behavior and goal setting. The experimental group differed from the control group in positive specific feedback, corrective specific feedback, and use of student'first names. They did not differ on variables such as teacher's acceptance of students'skill performance ideas, instruction/management time, positive general feedback, or positive corrective feedback.

Determining whether the effects of the intervention would generalize to another teaching setting in the same subject matter, and would be maintained over time was investigated by McKenzie (1981) in a case study. Target behaviors for change were: to decrease rates of using "OK", to increase rates of interacting with students by using their first names, and to increase rates of providing positive specific feedback. The intervention consisting of goal setting and feedback was effective in producing substantial changes. One year after, training effect was still lasting on the rate of "OK". The teacher continued to use the other target behavior at a higher rate than during baseline conditions but at a lower rate than during training.

Teacher enthusiasm is considered to be an important characteristic of effective teachers (Berliner & Tikunoff, 1976; Ryans, 1960). The construct of enthusiasm is much larger than one specific teaching skill. The question is also: Can we teach a student teacher to be enthusiastic in the gym?

Rolider (1979) defined nine classes of enthusiastic behavior: use of voice inflexion, use of gestures, smiling, laughing, teacher modeling behavior, use of physical contact, hustling, providing general positive feedback, use of positive prompts. Subjects were 15 preservice teachers. Rolider, Siedentop & Van Houten (1984) employed a multiple baseline across subjects design described as follows:

"After obtaining baseline data for all the 15 preservice teachers, the enthusiasm training program was introduced for six teachers while the remaining nine teachers remained in the baseline conditions. After the effects of the intervention on the performance of the first six teachers were assessed, the enthusiasm training program was introduced for four more of the teachers while the remaining five teachers continued in the baseline conditions. Finally the enthusiasm training program was also applied to the remaining five teachers" (Rolider, Siedentop & Van Houten, 1984).

Training consisted of seven two-hour training sessions during one-week period. It was based on explanation of the different enthusiastic behaviors and through the use of a systematic
videotape procedure. Subjects were able to increase significantly
in the use of verbal, non verbal and voice inflexion components
of enthusiastic behavior. It was also shown a clear relationship
between teacher enthusiasm and student motor engagement. Mean
percentage of time that at least half the class is engaged in
appropriate motor activity increased in 13 out of 15 subjects.

The effects of enthusiasm training has been also studied by
Carlisle & Phillips (1984) on 24 preservice physical education
majors enrolled in a 10-credit-hour program. The experimental
group followed a 6 hour enthusiasm training program. Teacher were
observed for enthusiasm, instruction time, and management time
during a 30-minute ETU. They were rated according to the 5-point
scale on eight qualities developed by Collins (1976). The short
term enthusiasm training experience increased significantly the
enthusiasm scores in the treatment group. However measures of
student motor engagement time did not differ between trained and
untrained groups. No significant correlation was found between
student engagement and enthusiasm score of the teachers.

PUPIL MOTOR ENGAGEMENT.

Motor engagement time or Academic Learning Time - Physical
Education (ALT-PE) was shown to be frequently in a positive
relationship with student achievement. It is easy to understand
that people involved in methods courses recommend sustained efforts as the key for high motor engagement time in a class. When
dealing with augmented feedback the intervention aims directly at
changing teacher behavior, for exemple: emitting more frequent
feedback and increasing positive feedback rate. Time spent on
task by students reflect numerous influences, teacher planning,
teaching interventions, methodology used, and student motivation.
With motor engagement time, the first thing to consider is to
modify some aspects of the teaching process located in the decision making domain of the teacher in such a way that the change
alters as a consequence of the student behavior and more specifically of motor engagement time.

Borys (1982, 1983, 1985) developed a training procedure to help secondary school physical education student teachers increase pupil motor engagement time. It was defined according to Laubach system (BESTPED) categories as the time students spent exercising, practicing and game playing.

A field test, using a pretest-posttest evaluation design, was carried out to assess the effects of the training procedure for increasing pupil motor engagement time. Eight student teachers participated in the field test. They taught a five-day basketball unit and re-taught this unit to a different class the following week. The training package included a workbook, a weekend seminar, and follow-up workshops. Treatment teachers (n = 4), as a group increased pupil motor engagement time to a greater extent than control group teachers. Although the intervention training procedure had a noticeable effect in helping the treatment group, to increase pupil motor engagement time, the impact on individual teachers varied considerably. In some instances, pupil motor engagement time decreased sharply after the intervention.

Several other studies attempted to increase ALT-PE in a school physical education setting through in-service training: instructional clinics, daily systematic feedback, pre-set criterion to meet, or by using behavior modification techniques.

Birdwell (1980) analyzed the effects of a package intervention on three in-service teachers at the elementary, junior high and senior high school levels. Dependent variables were management time, teacher feedback and student non-engagement time. Two additional variables (ALT-PE and ALP-PE(M) were not directly used as intervention variables but were analyzed by means of a concurrent baseline. The intervention was successful in facilitating a significant change in the three dependent variables. Significant increase of ALT-PE and of ALT-PE(M) were associated with decreases in teachers'management time, decreases in students not engaged in motor activity and increases in feedback provided to pupils. Hart (1983) used a similar design, a multiple baseline across behaviors, to show a relationship between the intervention and the behavior at each school involved in the study. It was observed that ALT-PE did increase from baseline through total intervention in three of the selected schools. In Beamer's study

(1983) the program to increase ALT-PE was successful in one school and not in a second school. Several additional findings in this study are worth looking at carefully: (1) Teacher behaviors did not seem to have much effect on ALT-PE; (2) Increasing teacher feedback to low-skilled students was not effective in increasing their ALT-PE proportionally more than for more highly-skilled students. The results of a study on the effects of a behavioral in-service model of supervision on the teaching effectiveness of teachers in terms of student motor engagement demonstrated only partial success in increasing or maintaining the amount of ALT-PE(M) (O'Sullivan, 1983).

TRAINING PROCEDURES.

The most common training procedures designed to change specific behaviors are as follows:

* Competency based modules written as instructions focusing upon various teaching skills. Modules include general goals, specific terminal behavioral goals, definitions of skills, suggestions for practicing those skills, available resources, and assessment procedure for the module.

* Terminal target goals in rates and percentages set for each teaching skill and for individual subjects.

* Cueing is a reminder in written or verbal form to work on the target teaching skills under intervention. It is delivered by a partner or by the investigator just prior to teaching a class.

* Verbal mediation requires subjects to cue themselves just before teaching by writing, saying, or reading over the specific target teaching skills and individual goals set on those skills. The trainee rehearses the teaching behaviors to be used prior to class time.

* Graphic and verbal feedback about the teaching skills performed in the class are given to each subject immediately after teaching, including whether or not the goal is reached and examples of use and nonuse of the teaching skills under supervision.

* Positive reinforcement given by a partner or by the investigator when improvements occurred in rate or percentages goals for teaching skills under intervention and on specific accomplishments.

Contingency management pointing out the relationship between the teaching behavior to be emitted and the consequence such as a passing grade in student teaching as a reward.

Reviewed studies evidenced that to some extent teaching behaviors can be changed in pre-service teachers as well as in-service teachers. Intervention procedures have usually been included in training packages because package grouping of several interventions was more efficient than the use of a unique type of intervention. Nevertheless, the purpose of several studies was to identify what kind of intervention was more likely to effect teaching behavior.

The effect of a cooperating teacher who modeled appropriate teaching behaviors was compared to the effect of written suggestions and feedback on an intern's teaching behavior (Douge, 1984). The study consisted of three single case systematic replications lasting for a ten-week period, divided into three weeks of pre-study and baseline measurement, four weeks of interventions, and three weeks of maintenance measurement. Three interns were in the control group. There were substantial changes in the target behaviors of the experimental student teachers. In the control group yet, few behaviors changed and none were lasting.

Joint supervision providing the student teacher with the opportunity to receive objective feedback from a peer, from a cooperating teacher, and from a university supervisor was observed to provide statistically significant differences between control and treatment groups (Reese, 1983).

Periodic prompting applied by wireless communication was investigated by van der Mars (1984). It was regarded as positive by subjects in building confidence through positive feedback, and in making them more aware of what occurred around them during teaching. On the contrary, being observed everyday became tiresome and being prompted to look elsewhere in the gym was found confusing. Periodic prompting did not increase several observational variables such as providing students with more informative feedback or using students'first names more frequently.

CONCLUSIONS.

Most of the studies focusing on changing specific teaching behaviors showed that these behaviors can be modified. Several intervention techniques or packages were efficient in attaining the objectives set by the investigator. Some changes lasted longer that other. Transfer of training must be considered with caution. It seems reasonable to state that changes cannot be considered definitive and that teachers are "condemned to a continuous search for improvement in their teaching abilities".

As far as variables like student time on task or motor engagement is concerned, we can abide to Borys (1983) statement:

"Because teaching in the gymnasium is a complex activity and teachers experience a multiplicity of settings, it is impossible for a training procedure to be too prescriptive. In addition pupil motor engagement time is influenced by variables other than those in the intervention package. These variables include the cooperating teacher, teaching style, pupil familiarity with subject matter, task difficulty, initial level of pupil motor engagement time, student teacher background, response to treatment, length and intensity of practice episodes, physical fitness levels, length of class, size of class and pupil motivation".

CHAPTER 8

CONCLUSIONS AND IMPLICATIONS

In the history of Education, theoreticians and great pedago-
gues have developed generous theories in relation to the whatever
philosophical and social systems they abide.

Curriculum theorists have made efforts to translate these
general theories into models and prescriptions for teachers.
However, they remain frequently apart from the daily practice in
the classroom, and in the gymnasium. Several authors like De
Landsheere (1976) in the classroom or Locke & Dodds (1984) and
Piéron (1978a) in the gymnasium underscored the gap existing
between theory and practice on the field.

Gage (1978) proposed that research on teaching occurs when
teacher behaviors serve as independent variables with some measure of pupil learning as the dependent variables. Locke used
this proposal to define the field : "Research on teaching physical education includes only studies which employ data gathered
through direct or indirect observation of instructional activity"
(Locke, 1977, p. 10).

Conclusions

In his challenging paper, Locke (1977) made a very critical assessment of the state of research in teaching physical education. It is extremely helpful to keep in mind his criticisms and his proposals to assess the actual state of the art, approximately ten years later.

> "Of greater import, however, such a definition would iden-
> tify some procedures not only as "not research on teaching"
> but also as "not research at all". Included here would be
> the most common form of research on teaching physical educa-
> tion, in which some innovative methodology is introduced and
> the subject to evaluation by measurement of student achieve-
> ment without any observation of the events through which the
> innovation was mediated - teaching. This kind of design has
> been the main source of obfuscation in teacher research
> throughout all areas of education for half a century"
> (Locke, 1977, p. 10).

Several objectives can characterize the research based on systematic observation of the classrooms or the gym: the desire to describe the reality of the class, the events happenning during a physical education lesson.

The studies based on observation and completed by now have implications at least at three levels:

(1) for the teacher;
(2) for those in charge of the teacher preparation;
(3) for researchers in pedagogy of physical education.

FOR TEACHERS.

In the last decade, specific areas' of research in teaching physical education have concentrated on the study and analysis of what happens during the teaching - learning process, in the gymnasium or on the sports field and has been based on a systematic observation of teacher behavior, student behavior, teacher - student interaction, and the contextual aspects of teaching. This research effort has provided sport pedagogy with invaluable descriptive data. It has led to a better understanding of the teaching act. It has helped methodologists to move beyond sole reliance on their subjective impressions and to base some of their recommendations on data derived from research rather than on unrealistic or romantic expectations from programmes (Siedentop, 1983a; Piéron, 1986).

The picture gained through observation of the teaching relationship showed that it does not necessarily meet the expectations of educational philosophy or curriculum theory or what could be expected in a subject matter devoted to human movement. It largely confirmed the gap between theory and practice.

Results of the analysis of teaching have allowed a profound reflection on the process of teaching, on what is occuring or, at least, what should be. These analyses have revealed:

* for teachers, accurate perception of their teaching behavior was not an easy task when confronted with instantaneous decisions and when surrounded by a continuous flow of events;

* the intra-individual variability of teaching behaviors seemed to be far less extensive than teachers have affirmed. Several studies showed that the whole teacher - student interaction varied very little in the short or long term. Several contextual variables seemed to influence only moderately the teaching behaviors or the teaching functions. This seems to be the case with teacher augmented feedback as well.

When the analysis is superceding the purely descriptive and entering the correlational aspect of the descriptive - correlational - experimental loop described by Rosenshine & Furst (1973), two variables appeared to play a prominant role in teaching effectiveness: the student motor engagement and the information provided to the student as feedback following his or her motor performance. These two variables are probably related. They depend on other teaching functions such as organization and management of the class.

We must be cautious not to be trapped into a reductionnist view and use these variables as starting points for devising evaluation instruments. It must be kept in mind that their relationship with the student achievement, or student learning gains is not linear. We face a relationship shaped as an inverted U.

Conclusions

That means that too much or too little importance devoted to one of these variables could be detrimental and could induce counter-effects on student outcomes.

It must be remembered that these variables have been identified in simplified settings like experimental teaching units (ETU), and that the learning objectives dealt with in ETU's are not the only objectives to be pursued in physical education.

In general terms, two specific moments are due to influence teaching effectiveness. They concern on the one hand pre-active decisions made before meeting with students and, on the other hand, decisions made when the teacher interacts with the students and when the setting and the interaction are constinuously moving (the active phase of teaching).

First decisions taken by teachers concern the choice of objectives, the assessment of students needs and skills, the analysis of the activities proposed to match objectives, needs, and aptitudes of the students, the selection of the organization and the management of the class, and the use of the most appropriate teaching style.

While the pre-active phase has prominent importance to the success of teaching, any failure during the active phase of teaching renders all this pre-active phase worthless. Absence or carelessness in preparing the instruction endangers the action and consequently the outcome. Decisions made during the two phases must play complementary roles.

Although the information provided in the text concerns almost essentially what is happening during the class, the reader must keep in mind the indispensable relationship between the pre-active and the active part of teaching activities.

Important data gathered in research in classroom teaching can be briefly summarized. Effective teachers are those who are able to maintain their students appropriately involved and on task during a large part of the allocated time without using negative or coercive methods. The components of teaching effectiveness could be:

Conclusions

* a large proportion of time devoted to the subject matter taught;

* a high rate of behaviors directly related to the learning tasks;

* an adequate matching of the content of teaching with students abilities;

* the development of a positive climate in the classroom.

When transfering findings from studies completed in the classroom setting, it must be clearly stated that striking differences exist between classroom teaching aimed at the acquisition of knowledge by students seated or gathered in a closed space like a classroom and a subject matter whose objective is to enjoy physical activities with the students free to move in largely open spaces. However, several findings in both settings converged inconclusion.

Let us consider what is happening in physical education teaching and whether criteria from classroom teaching are applicable in physical education and sport activities.

Besides the knowledge gathered in the classroom, implications of the research in teaching for physical education teachers arise from several sources:

* Comparison of behaviors of master teachers, beginning teachers and students teachers.

* Findings collected from the experimental teaching units (ETU). The ETU describes teacher and student behaviors during the instruction periods and pupil learning outcomes. Generalization of the results must be made carefully. ETUs are simplified situations from the complexity of the teaching phenomenon. However, they show enough similarities to allow large inferences from their results and to apply these findings in daily teaching practice. They can be compared to teaching as a gamelike situation of 3 on 3 played on a half basketball court can be compared to a full court basketball game. It is not complete basketball but most of the skills necessary for a top level basketball

players can be demonstrated and practiced in a 3 on 3 gamelike situation. To give more validity to the data collected in ETU studies it must be underscored that there is presently a trend to use longer periods of instruction and intact classes in the process-product studies using the ETU model.

Findings from the above mentioned research on the process of teaching coalesce with four groups of variables that seem to play a meaningful role in the success of teaching physical education: time spent by students in practicing physical activities, augmented feedback provided by teachers to students, the organization, and the climate of the class.

1. STUDENT MOTOR ENGAGEMENT. It concerns the amount of time effectively spent in practicing physical activities during the periods allocated to physical activities by the school policies. Results of our process-product studies tend to show that to be relevant to student outcomes, time must be devoted to the practice of task related and at a high rate of success. These findings are in general agreement with data from the classroom research. Time spent on task is considered as a mediator between instruction and teacher intervention on the one hand and on the other hand student, learning gains.

2. A POSITIVE CLASS CLIMATE. Amongst the many physical education teaching objectives, one aims at emphasizing a desire for participation in out-of-school physical activities, especially after the scholarly enterprise has ended. A positive attitude towards physical activities will develop only if participants have succeeded in acquiring sports skills and if they have enjoyed taking part in physical activities in a supportive climate created, especially by the physical education teacher.

3. FREQUENT AND QUALITY INFORMATION ON STUDENT PERFORMANCE. In motor learning feedback is considered an important key issue. It is frequently limited to the sole concept of knowledge of results, considered as reinforcement, and provisive of information on the correctness or incorrectness of the student performance. Continuous progress seems to be impossible without more complete information. In teaching, information about performance easily exceeds the simple information limited to success or

failure. It intends to provide the student with the means to improve performance. It can help in discovering ways to insure improvement. Feedback could be considered to be at the crossroads of two complementary phenomena: teaching and learning. Let us add that providing information on student performance correlates with the concern of the student in search for excellence.

4. THE ORGANIZATION OF THE CLASS ACTIVITIES. Maximizing individual motor engagement, as well as providing frequent good quality feedback, cannot be envisaged unless the conditions for practicing physical activities are carefully planned and organized. Such an organization facilitates the management of the class and eases discipline problems.

In summary, it is crucial that the teacher increases opportunities for the student to be involved in physical activities, provides the students with more informative feedback and generate a climate emphasizing praise and positive approach. These three objectives cannot be met without a careful organization of the class.

In the teacher - student relationship, two other concepts must be taken into account: the aptitude - treatment interaction and teacher expectancy. Careful consideration confirms a more accurate coverage of the different elements of the teaching act already identified.

(1) the aptitude - treatment interaction relates to different reactions from a student towards the same intervention. All personalities attending the same class do not react similarly to the same intervention or the same activity proposed by the teacher.

(2) Observations and analyses allowed us to quantify differences between students involved in the same class. Systematic observation of high and low achievers has shown that student motor engagement and the success in performing tasks alone tended to widen the differences between students. Without conscious and effective intervention from the teacher, the gap between these type of students will tend to increase dramatically.

Conclusions

FOR THOSE WHOSE MISSION IS TO PREPARE TEACHERS.

Analysis of teaching in physical education provides us with some sound basis to prepare teachers and to be less subjective.

The modification of the whole teaching relationship seems to be difficult to achieve merely by studying a system of systematic observation and mastering skill attempts. Many studies centered on changing specific teaching interventions and teaching strategies showed clearly that teachers were able to master them. The mastering of teaching skills is not the sole province of chance learning.

However, any newly learned or modified behavior does not necessarily remain at the level attained during intervention. It tends to return progressively towards its baseline level. This fact means that every teacher, like all "responsible citizen" is condemned to a continuous search for improvement to prevent falling into a routine that debilitates the educational opportunities of students.

Studies dealing with teaching skills acquisition through specific interventions have shown that they are just as applicable in pre-service preparation as in-service training. Specific interventions are able to provide better individualized preparation. To be fully efficient intervention strategies must be combined in packages including micro-teaching, informative feedback, competency-based objectives, and performance criteria programs.

People in charge of teacher preparation can benefit from teaching analysis for:

* defining more accurately teaching behaviors and the strategies needing for mastering and

* involving more deeply the student-teacher in his or her own project; self analysis and working with peers has produced more substantial and enduring improvements.

Conclusions

FOR RESEARCHERS.

During the last decade the research on what is occuring in a physical education classrooms has shifted from embrionic status to one of enthusiastic youth, sometimes a little disorderly and lacking in continuity, but creative and concerned with the magnitude and the multitude of questions involved.

Remarkable results have been achieved. Research in teaching physical education has developed reliable and valid observation instruments dealing with general and different specific aspects of the teaching act. A catalog of instruments has been published (Darst, Mancini & Zakrajsek, 1983). It was one of the Locke's proposals (Locke, 1977).

The remarkable Video Data Bank Project of Teachers College, Columbia University gave birth to many offsprings in the USA as well as in other part of the world and provided researchers with data for continuous study. A project to share tapes from these video data collections could be a great achievement as well. That is also one of the tasks proposed by Locke (1977).

However, the descriptive - correlational - experimental loop refered to by Rosenshine and Furst (1973) is far from being completed in the physical education teaching research. Many examples of the first step, the descriptive approach can be found. But few examples of the second and the third steps, the correlational and experimental paradigms, in research in teaching physical education have yet appeared.

The opportunities to generalize the implications of research findings is high in several areas, but must be greatly increased in others. It has been pointed out in final report of the Olympic Scientific Congress about half of the studies (47.7%) reviewed by Piéron (1986) focused on observation of in-service teachers, i.e. persons already trained. The picture gained through teaching analysis seemed therefore to represent the daily reality of the school compared to information gathered through student - teacher observation (24.1%). A student-teacher may well change his or her teaching patterns between graduation and the field practice. Findings provide three types of highly necessary data for a sound knowledge of teaching skills which can be used to improve teacher preparation: knowing where the trainee is coming from (student-teacher), where he or she has the greater chances to go (in-service teachers) and where it is worth going (master teachers).

Nevertheless, it was amazing to observe that 60.2% of the studies did not provide the reader with sufficient information even to identify the subject matter taught. This proportion is particularly high in interaction analysis studies (93.4%). The only area where the subject matter is always clearly described is process - product studies. Some problems obtained with the studies as they tend to project a simplistic product, but certainly they relate to subject matter. Grouping data from different activities could have been tolerated in the early studies when searching for an initial understanding of the teaching process. It is unwise to continue with such a practice now.

The achievement of this research is still limited to the description of what is occuring in the class in different context settings dealing primarily with the influence of the grade and the school level, and the gender. The influence of programme variables like subject matter taught, the objectives aimed at by the teacher, and the teaching methods, indicate that teacher planning needs to be studied more extensively. Because teachers have more decision - making power in programme variables than in contextual variables, further improvement of the actual body of knowledge must be made in focusing on the programme variables rather than on context variables.

Description has been largely quantitative. We know well how much feedback is delivered, the amount of student motor engage-ment and, other characteristics of student participation. The purely quantitative analyses of data can be seen as lacking in flexibility, in information on the quality of the event, and of the adequacy of teacher interventions. Quantitative data are still necessary, but they must be complemented by qualitative information.

Information gathered by observation will become more useful when complemented by more multidimensional input. A question to illustrate: does feedback emitted by the teacher correspond to the error identified with the performer ? Does it deal with primary ou secondary errors ?

Conclusions

Focusing on a single aspect of the events occuring in the class, either in teacher behavior or in student engagement is limited as far as the interpretation of data is concerned. Teacher and student behaviors must be studied in harmony. Multivariate data must be collected and observation can be linked to psychological and physiological data.

The flexibility of teacher behavior or its counterpart, the stability of teacher behavior, is largely unknown. Studies in this area must be continued for teacher training purposes as well as for evaluation purposes.

Many populations need still to be studied. Some data on the teaching relationship exist in mainstreamed classes or with handicapped children. However the scope is still very limited.

So far, most of the studies are unique. Very few have been replicated in similar or comparable conditions. Longitudinal studies could provide data usable in teacher preparation.

The pre-active decisions and those occuring during the active phase of teaching must be tackled by observation and by investigation of the decision making processes followed by the teacher.

Doors have been opened to develop process - product studies, and to link quantitative observation with qualitative appraisal.

Optimistic views on teaching research can be expressed in the sense that in a few short years career researchers in physical education have become involved in research on teaching and that some programmatic research has permitted development of a cumulative body of knowledge.

REFERENCES

AKKANEN, O. (1979). Use of different teaching patterns based on the analysis of verbal behavior and collective movement activity / passivity of pupils in P.E. classes of junior comprehensive school teachers. In T. Tammivuori (Ed.), Evaluation. International congress of physical education, July 1976. Helsinki, Finnish society for research in sport and physical education, Publication nr 64, 89-96.

ALEXANDER, K. (1982). Behavior Analysis of Tasks and Accountability in Physical Education. Unpublished doctoral dissertation. Ohio State University.

ALEXANDER, K. (1983). Beyond the prediction of student achievement: direct and repeated measurement of behavior change. In P. Dodds & F. Rife (Eds), Time to learn in physical education: History, completed research, and potential future for Academic Learning Time in physical education, Monograph 1, 42-47.

ALLARD, R. (1979). Teacher behavior directed towards individual students in physical education classes: the influence of student gender and class participation. Unpublished doctoral dissertation, University of Massachusetts.

ANDERSON, H.H. (1939). The measurement of domination and of socially integrative behavior in teacher's contacts with children, Child development, 10, 73-89.

ANDERSON, W. (1971). Descriptive-analytic research on teaching. Quest, 15, 1-8.

ANDERSON, W. (1975). Videotape data bank, Journal of physical education, & recreation, 46, 7, 31-35.

References

ANDERSON, W. (1978). Introduction. In, W. Anderson, & G. Barrette (Eds), What's going on in gym: descriptive studies of physical education classes. Monograph 1, Motor skills: theory into practice, 1-10.

ANDERSON, W. (1980). Analysis of teaching physical education. St Louis: C.V. Mosby.

ANDERSON, W. (1983a). Physical Education Teachers Professional Functions. In, P. Darst, V. Mancini, & D. Zakrajsek (Eds), Systematic Observation Instrumentation for Physical Education. West Point: Leisure Press, 275-295.

ANDERSON, W. (1983b). Observations from outside the system. In P. Dodds, & F. Rife (Eds), Time to learn in physical education: History, completed research, and potential future for Academic Learning Time in physical education, Monograph 1, 53-59.

ANDERSON, W., & BARRETTE, G. (1978a). What's going on in gym: descriptive studies of physical education classes. Motor skills: Theory into practice, monograph 1, 1978.

ANDERSON, W., & BARRETTE, G. (1978b). Teacher behavior. In, W. Anderson, & G. Barrette (Eds), What's going on in gym: descriptive studies of physical education classes. Monograph 1, Motor skills: theory into practice, 25-38.

ANDERSON, W., & BARRETTE, G. (1980). Teacher behavior in physical education classes. In, G. Schilling, & W. Baur (Eds), Audiovisuelle Medien im Sport. Moyens audiovisuels dans le sport. Audiovisual means in sports. Basel, Birkhauser Verlag, 255-276.

ARENA, L. (1979). Descriptive and experimental studies of augmented instructional feedback in sport settings. Unpublished doctoral dissertation, Ohio State University.

ARMSTRONG, C. (1977). Teaching experience, knowledge of performer competency and performance outcome as determinants of proficiency in performance error identification. Unpublished doctoral dissertation, Pittsburgh University.

References

ARMSTRONG, C., & HOFFMANN,S. (1979). Effects of teaching experience, knowledge of performer competence, and knowledge of performance outcome on performance error identification. Research Quarterly, 50, 318-327.

AUFDERHEIDE, S. (1980). Individualized teaching strategies in mainstreamed physical education classes and their relationship to academic learning time. Unpublished doctoral dissertation, University of Texas at Austin.

AUFDERHEIDE, S. (1983). ALT-PE in Mainstreamed Physical Education Classes. In P. Dodds, & F. Rife (Eds), Time to learn in physical education: History, completed research, and potential future for Academic Learning Time in physical education, Monograph 1, 22-26.

AUFDERHEIDE, S., McKENZIE, T., & KNOWLES, C. (1982). Effect of individualized instruction of handicapped and nonhandicapped students in elementary physical education classes. Journal of Teaching in Physical Education, 1, 3, 51-57.

BAHNEMAN, C. (1971). An analysis of the relationship between selected personality characteristics and the verbal behavior of physical education teachers. Unpublished doctoral dissertation, University of Pittsburgh.

BAILEY, L. (1982). Microteaching and teaching of games. Carnegie Research Papers, 1, 4, 33-35.

BAIN, L. (1974). Description and analysis of the hidden curriculum in physical education. Unpublished doctoral dissertation, University of Wisconsin.

BAIN, L. (1976a). Description of the hidden curriculum in secondary physical education. Research Quarterly, 47, 154-160.

BAIN, L. (1976b). An instrument for identifying implicit values in physi-cal education programs. Research Quarterly, 47, 307-314.

BAIN, L. (1978). Differences in values implicit in teaching and coaching behaviors. Research Quarterly, 49, 6-11.

References

BAIN, L. (1983a). Teacher / coach role conflict: Factors influencing role performance. In, T. Templin, & J. Olson (Eds),
Teaching in Physical Education. Champaign: Human Kinetics, 94-
101.

BAIN, L. (1983b). Implicit Values Instrument for Physical Edu-
cation (IVI-PE). In, P. Darst, V. Mancini, & D. Zakrajsek (Eds),
Systematic Observation Instrumentation for Physical Education.
West Point: Leisure Press, 329-352.

BARRETT, K. (1969). A procedure for systematically describing
teacher-student behavior in primary physical education lessons
implementing the concept of movement education. Unpublished doctoral dissertation, University of Wisconsin.

BARRETT, K. (1971). The structure of movement tasks - a means
for gaining insight into the nature of problem - solving techniques. Quest, 15, 22-31.

BARRETT, K. (1979a). Observation for teaching and coaching.
Journal of Physical Education and Recreation, 50, 1, 23-25.

BARRETT, K. (1979b). Observation of movement for teachers - A
synthesis and implications. Motor Skills: Theory into Practice,
3, 2, 67-76.

BARRETT, K. (1983). A hypothetical model of observing as a
teaching skill. Journal of Teaching in physical education, 3, 1,
22-31.

BARRETTE, G. (1977). A descriptive analysis of teacher behavior
in physical education classes. Unpublished doctoral dissertation,
Teachers College, Columbia University.

BATCHELDER, A. (1975). Process objectives and their implementa-
tion in elementary math, English, and physical education classes.
Unpublished doctoral dissertation, Boston University.

BATCHELDER, A., & CHEFFERS, J. (1978). CAFIAS: an interaction
analysis instrument for observing verbal and non verbal behaviors
in learning settings. In F. Landry, & W. Orban (Eds), International congress of physical activity sciences. Motor learning, sport

psychology pedagogy and didactics of physical activity. Miami, Symposia specialists. Vol. 7, 433-442.

BATCHELDER, A., & KEANE, F. (1983). Batchelder - Keane Lecture System (BAKE). In, P. Darst, V. Mancini, & D. Zakrajsek (Eds), Systematic Observation Instrumentation for Physical Education. West Point: Leisure Press, 106-108.

BEAMER, D. (1983). The effects of an inservice education program on the academic learning time of selected students in physical education. Unpublished doctoral dissertation, Ohio State University.

BENJAMIN, L. (1977). The effect of inner-city and suburban settings on attitudinal and behavioral characteristics of preservice physical educa-tion teachers. Unpublished doctoral dissertation, Temple University.

BENNETT, N. (1978). Recent research on teaching: a dream, a belief, and a model. Journal of Education, 160, 3, 5-37.

BERLINER, D. (1979). Tempus educare. In, P. Peterson, & H. Walberg (Eds), Research on Teaching: Concepts, Findings and Implications. Berkeley, Calif.: Mc Cutchan, 120-135.

BERLINER, D., & TIKUNOFF, W. (1976). The California beginning teacher evaluation study. Journal of teacher education, 27, 1, 24-30.

BIRDWELL, D. (1980). The effects of modification of teacher behavior on selected students in physical education. Unpublished doctoral dissertation, Ohio State University.

BLOMM, B. (1979). Caractéristiques individuelles et apprentissages scolaires. Bruxelles, Ed. Labor.

BOCHMAN, J., HEIDUK, N., & ULLRICH, (1975). Einige Analyseergebnisse zur Sprache des Lehrers im Sportunterricht. Körpererziehung, 25, 231-234.

References

BOEHM, J. (1974). The effects of a competency - based teaching program on junior high school physical education student teachers and their pupils. Unpublished doctoral dissertation, Ohio State University.

BOOKHOUT, E. (1966). An observational study of teaching behavior in relation to the socio-emotional climate of physical education classes. Unpublished doctoral dissertation, New York University.

BOOKHOUT, E. (1967). Teaching behavior in relation to the socio emotional climate of physical education classes. Research Quarterly, 38, 336-347.

BORYS, A. (1982). Development and evaluation of a training procedure to increase pupil motor engagement time. Unpublished doctoral dissertation, Teachers College, Columbia University.

BORYS, A. (1983). Increasing pupil motor engagement time: case studies of student teachers. In, R. Telama, V. Varstala, J. Tiainen, L. Laakso, & T. Haajanen (Eds), Research in school physical education. Jyvaskyla: The foundation for promotion of physical culture and health, 351-358.

BORYS, A. (1986). Development of a Training Procedure to Increase Pupil Motor Engagement Time (MET). In, M. Piéron, & G. Graham (Ed.), The 1984 Olympic Scientific Comgress Proceedings, Vol. 6, Sport Pedagogy, Champaign: Human Kinetics, 19-25.

BRESSANE, R. (1982). Perfil de ensino atraves de sistema FaMOC. Communidade esportiva, 3, 19, 1982, 20-23.

BROWN, J. (1980). A description of student/teacher dyadic interactions in physical activity classes. Unpublished doctoral dissertation, University of North Carolina at Greensboro.

BRUNELLE, J. (1973). Utilisation du système de Joyce dans la formation des stagiaires (éducation physique). In, Dussault G., & coll. (Eds), L'analyse de l'enseignement. Montréal, Presses Université du Québec, 261-280.

References

BRUNELLE, J. (1975). Un système d'analyse de présentation de cours en éducation physique. Unpublished doctoral dissertation, University of Liege, 1975.

BRUNELLE, J., & de CARUFEL, F. (1982). Analyse des feedback émis par des maîtres de l'enseignement de la danse moderne. Revue Québecoise de l'activité physique, 2, 3-8.

BRUNELLE, J., GODBOUT, P., DROUIN, D., DESHARNAIS, R., LORD, M., & TOUSIGNANT, M. (1980). Rapport de recherche sur la qualité de l'intervention en éducation physique. Québec, Université Laval, Département d'éducation physique.

BRUNELLE, J., GODBOUT, P., TOUSIGNANT, M., BRUNELLE, J.P., & TRUDEL, P. (1985). Relations entre les habiletés initiales, les temps d'apprentissage et les gains réalisés par les participants. Revue Québecoise de l'Activité Physique, 3, 3, 92-100.

BRUNELLE, J., PIERON, M., & TOUSIGNANT, M. (1981). Student teachers'perceptions of cooperating teachers effectiveness. Journal of Teaching in Physical Education, Introductory Issue, 80-87.

BRUNELLE, J., SPALANZANI, C., LORD, M., & PETIOT, B. (1983). Analyse du climat pédagogique par le biais des réactions des éducateurs physiques en situation d'enseignement. Revue de l'ACSEPR, suppl. mars, 15-18 & 30.

BRUNELLE, J., TALBOT, S., TOUSIGNANT, M., & BERUBE, G. (1976). Comment les instructeurs de hockey enseignent. Québec, Université Laval.

BRUNELLE, J., TALBOT, S., TOUSIGNANT, M., HUBERT, M., & OUELLET, C. (1978a). Présentation d'un système d'analyse ayant pour objet de vérifier la capacité des instructeurs de hockey à appliquer des principes pédagogiques dans leur enseignement. In, F. Landry, & W. Orban (Eds), International congress of physical activity sciences. Motor learning, sport psychology pedagogy and didactics of physical activity. Miami, Symposia specialists. Vol. 7, 451-457.

BRUNELLE, J., TALBOT, S., TOUSIGNANT, M., HUBERT, M., & OUELLET, C. (1978b). Inventaire du comportement pédagogique des instructeurs de hockey sur glace en situation d'enseignement dans une perspective de supervision. In, F. Landry, & W. Orban (Eds), International congress of physical activity sciences. 10, International symposium on research and development in ice hockey. Miami, Symposia specialists, 133-138.

CARLIER, G., & ANDREANI, A. (1980). Contrôle des informations verbales de l'enseignement en éducation physique dans le cadre d'une expérience en pédagogie expérimentale au moyen de la technique de Joyce et d'une analyse de contenu. In, G. Schilling,& W. Baur (Eds), Audiovisuelle Medien im Sport. Moyens audiovisuels dans le sport. Audiovisual means in sports. Basel, Birkhauser Verlag, 356-360.

CARLISLE, P. (1981). An analysis of the relationships between selected teacher process variables, selected skill learning time variables, and student achievement in physical education classes, grades five through eigth. Unpublished doctoral dissertation, University of Colorado at Boulder.

CARLISLE, C., & PHILLIPS, A. (1984). The effects of enthusiasm training on selected teacher and student behaviors in preservice physical education teachers. Journal of Teaching in Physical Education, 4, 1, 64-75.

CARROLL, J., (1963). A model of school learning. Teachers College Record, 64, 723-733.

CARUSO, V. (1980). Behaviors indicating teacher enthusiasm, critical incidents reported by teachers and students in secondary school physical education and English classes. Unpublished doctoral dissertation , University of Massachussets.

CATELLI, L. (1979). Verbal and non verbal moves in teaching: a descriptive system for the analysis of teaching physical education. Unpublished doctoral dissertation, Teachers College, Columbia University, New York.

CHEFFERS, J. (1973). The validation of an instrument designed to expand the Flanders system of interaction analysis to describe non-verbal interaction, different varieties of teacher behaviour

References

and pupil responses. Unpublished doctoral dissertation, Temple University.

CHEFFERS, J. (1978). Systematic observation in teaching. In, M. Piéron (Ed), Towards a science of teaching: Teaching analysis. Liège: AIESEP, 7-30.

CHEFFERS, J. (1983). Cheffers'Adaptation of the Flanders'Inter-action Analysis System (CAFIAS). In, P. Darst, V. Mancini, & D. Zakrajsek (Eds), Systematic Observation Instrumentation for Physical Education. West Point: Leisure Press, 76-96.

CHEFFERS, J., & MANCINI, V. (1978). Teacher-student inter-action. In, W. Anderson, & G. Barrette (Eds), What's going on in gym: descriptive studies of physical education classes. Monograph 1, Motor skills: theory into practice, 39-50.

CHEFFERS, J., BRUNELLE, J., & VON KELSCH, R. (1980). Measuring student involvement. In, G. Schillings, & W. Baur (Eds), Audio-visuelle Medien im Sport. Moyens audiovisuels dans le sport. Audiovisual means in sports. Basel, Birkhauser Verlag, 1980, 216-229.

CHEFFERS, J., MANCINI, V., & MARTINEK, T. (1980). Interaction analysis: an application to non verbal activity, (2d Ed). St. Paul, Minnesota: Paul S. Amidon & Associates, Assn for productive teaching.

CHEFFERS, J., & WUEST, D. (1983). Individual Reaction Gestalt, Second Edition (IRG II), In, Darst, P., Mancini, V., & Zakrajsek, D. (Eds), Systematic Observation Instrumentation for Physical Education. West Point, Leisure Press, 118-124.

CHRISTENSON, R. (1983). Christenson analytic system for coding teacher behavior in physical education: a descriptive system of evaluation using a microcomputer (CASTEB). Unpublished doctoral dissertation, Brigham Young University.

COLE, J. (1979). A descriptive analysis of teacher augmented feedback given to university students in beginning golf classes. Unpublished docto-ral dissertation, University of North Carolina at Greensboro.

References

COLLINS, M. (1976). The effects of training for enthusiasm on the enthusiasm diplayed by preservice elementary teachers. Doctoral dissertation, Syracuse University, Dissertation Abstracts International, 37, 11, 7083 A.

COSTELLO, J. (1977). A descriptive analysis of students behaviors in elementary school physical education classes. Unpublished doctoral disserta-tion, Columbia University.

COSTELLO, J. , & LAUBACH, S. (1978), Student behavior. In, W. Anderson et G. Barrette (Eds), What's going on in gym: descriptive studies. Motor Skills: theory into practice, monograph 1, 11-24.

COUNTISS, J.R. (1976). The effects of training in the spectrum of teaching styles on the attitudes and classroom behavior of inservice physical education teachers. Unpublished doctoral dissertation, Temple University.

CRAFT, A. (1977). The teaching of skills for the observation of movement: Inquiry into a model. Unpublished doctoral dissertation, University of North Carolina at Greensboro.

CRAMER, C. (1977). The effects of a cooperating teacher training program in applied behavior analysis on selected teacher behaviors of secondary physical education student teachers. Unpublished doctoral dissertation, Ohio State University.

CURRENS, J. (1977). An applied behavior analysis training model for preservice teachers. Unpublished doctoral dissertation, Ohio State University.

DARST, P. (1974). The effect of a competency-based intervention of student teacher and pupil behavior. Unpublished doctoral dissertation, Ohio State University.

DARST, P. (1976). Effects of competency - based intertention on student teacher and pupil behavior. Research Quarterly, 47, 336-345.

DARST, P., MANCINI, V., & ZAKRAJSEK, D. (1983). Use of Interaction Analysis System. In, P. Darst, V. Mancini, & D. Zakrajsek

References

(Eds), Systematic Observation Instrumentation for Physical Education. West Point: Leisure Press, 12-28.

DE KNOP, P. (1983a). Effectiveness of tennis teaching. In, R. Telama, V. Varstala, J. Tiainen, L. Laakso, & T. Haajanen (Eds), Research in school physical education. Jyvaskyla: The foundation for promotion of physical culture and health, 228-234.

DE KNOP, P (1983b). Onderzoek naar enkele bepalende factoren van efficient lesgeversgedrag by tennisinitiatielessen. Unpublished doctoral dissertation, Vrije Universiteit Brussel.

DE KNOP, P. (1986). Relationship of Specified Instructional Teacher Behaviors to Student Gain on Tennis. Journal of Teaching in Physical Education, 5, 2, 71-78.

DE LANDSHEERE, G. (1976). Introduction à la recherche en éducation. Liège: Thone.

DE LANDSHEERE, G., & BAYER, E. (1974). Comment les maîtres enseignent. Bruxelles, Ministère de l'Education nationale.

DEMARTEAU, M., & PIERON, M. (1978). Analyse des communications verbales entre un professeur d'éducation physique et ses élèves. In M. Piéron (Ed.), Towards a science of teaching: Teaching analysis. Liège: AIESEP, 98-124.

De PAEPE, J. (1985). The Influence of Three Least Restrictive Environments on the Content Motor-ALT and Performance of Moderately Mentally Retarded Students. Journal of Teaching in Physical Education, 5, 1, 34-41.

DESSECKER, W. (1975). The effects of audio taped intervention on student behavior. Unpublished doctoral dissertation, Ohio State University.

DEVLIN, G., MANCINI, V., & FRYE, P. (1981). Teaching contingency manage-ment skills to disruptive elem students: effects on student self-concept and physical educators'behaviors. Journal of teaching in physical educa-tion, 1, 1, 47-58.

References

DOBRY, L., & SVATON, V. (1977). Analysis of teacher instructional activities in physical education. Praha, University Karlova, 63-106.

DODDS, P. (1975). A behavioral competency-based peer assessment model for student teacher supervision in elementary physical education. Unpublished doctoral dissertation, Ohio State University.

DODDS, P. (1978). Behavior Analysis of Students: What Students can Tell Teachers Without Ever Saying a Word. Motor Skills: Theory into Practice, 3, 3-10.

DODDS, P. (1979). A peer assessment model for the student teacher supervision. Research Quarterly, 50, 18-29.

DODDS, P. (1983a). Relationship between academic learning time and teacher behaviors in a physical education majors skills class. In, T. Templin, & J. Olson (Eds), Teaching in Physical Education. Champaign: Human Kinetics, 173-184.

DODDS, P. (1983b). Student Teachers Observing Peers (STOP). In, P. Darst, V. Mancini, & D. Zakrajsek (Eds), Systematic Observation Instrumentation for Physical Education. West Point: Leisure Press, 140-154.

DODDS, P., RIFE, F., & METZLER, M. (1982). Academic learning time in physical education: data collection, completed research and future directions. In, Piéron, M., & Cheffers, J. (Eds), Studying the teaching in physical education: AIESEP, 37-51.

DODDS, P., & RIFE, F. (1983). Time to learn in physical education: History, completed research, and potential future for Academic Learning Time in physical education, Monograph 1, 42-47.

DOUGE, B. (1984). The effect of a cooperating teacher's modeling of specific teaching behaviors on the teaching behavior of a physical education international unpublished doctoral dissertation, Ohio State University.

DOUGHERTY, N. (1970). A comparison of the effects of command, task and individual program styles of teaching in the development of physical fitness and motor skills. Unpublished doctoral dissertation, Temple University.

DOUGHERTY, N. (1971). A plan for the analysis of teacher - pupil interaction in physical education classes. Quest, 15, 39-49.

DOUGHERTY, N. (1983). Adaptation of the Flanders System of Interaction Analysis. In, P. Darst, V. Mancini, & D. Zakrajsek (Eds), Systematic Observation Instrumentation for Physical Education. West Point: Leisure Press, 29-33.

DUSSAULT, G., LECLERC, M., BRUNELLE, J., & TURCOTTE, C. (1973). L'analyse de l'enseignement. Montréal, Presses de l'Université du Québec.

EGGER, K. (1980). Unterrichtsbeobachtung im Sportunterricht. Ein Seminarbericht ueber die Entwicklung eines Analyseinstruments. In, G. Schillings, & W. Baur (Eds), Audiovisuelle Medien im Sport. Moyens audiovisuels dans le sport. Audiovisual means in sports. Basel, Birkhauser Verlag, 340-355.

ERBANI, E. (1982). Influence de l'expérience sportive de compétition sur la pratique des étudiants en e.p.s., Motricité Humaine, 1, 3-11.

EWENS, B. (1981). Effects of self-assessment and goal setting on verbal behavior of elementary physical education teachers. Unpublished doctoral dissertation, Arizona State University.

EWERS, J. (1981). A study using Flanders interaction analysis to determine teacher-student communication patterns in selected urban elementary school physical education classes. Unpublished doctoral dissertation, University of Massachusetts.

FISHER, C., MANCINI, V., HIRSCH, R., PROULX, R., & STAUROWSKY, E. (1982). Coach-athlete interactions and team climate. Journal of Sport Psychology, 4: 388-404.

FISHMAN, S. (1974). A procedure for recording augmented feedback in physical education classes. Unpublished doctoral dissertation, Teachers College, Columbia University.

References

FISHMAN, S., & ANDERSON, W. (1971). Developing a system for describing teaching. Quest, 15, 9-16.

FISHMAN, S., & TOBEY, C. (1978). Augmented feedback. In, W. Anderson, & G. Barrette (Eds), What's going on in gym: descriptive studies. Motor skills: theory into practice, monograph 1, 51-62.

FLANDERS, N. (1970). Analyzing teaching behavior. Reading, Mass: Addison Wesley Pub. Cy.

FREEDMAN, M. (1978). Follow-up of physical education graduates from a teacher preparation program: a descriptive analysis. Unpublished doctoral dissertation, Ohio State University.

GAGE, N. (1968). An analytic approach to research on instructional methods. Phi Delta Kappan, 49, 601-606.

GAGE, N. (1972). Teacher Effectiveness and Teacher Education. Palo Alto: Pacific Books.

GAGE, N. (1978). The scientific basis of the art of teaching. New York: Teachers College Press.

GAUTHIER, A. (1980). A descriptive - analytic study of teacher-student interaction in mainstreamed physical education classes. Unpublished dissertation, Purdue University.

GENTILE, A. (1972). A working model of skill acquisition with application to teaching. Quest, 17, 3-23.

GODBOUT, P., BRUNELLE, J., & TOUSIGNANT, M. (1983). Academic learning time in elementary and secondary physical education classes. Research Quarterly for Exercise and Sport, 54, 1, 11-19.

GOLDBERGER, M. (1983b). The Behavior Analysis Tool (BAT). In, P. Darst, V. Mancini, & D. Zakrajsek (Eds), Systematic Observation Instrumentation for Physical Education. West Point: Leisure Press, 70-75.

GOMES de FARIA, J. (1980). Une contribution à l'étude du comportement verbal du professeur d'éducation physique. Proposition

References

du système FaMOC d'analyse d'enseignement. Unpublished doctoral dissertation, University of Brussels.

GONCALVES, C., & PIERON, M. (1986). A relaçao entre professor e praticantes em dois contextos diferentes: escola e clube. Uma analise em basquetebol. In, Congresso SPEF e Universidade Tecnica de Lisboa, Motricidade e Desenvolvimento. Lisboa: ISEF/UTL, 139-153.

GOOD, T., & BROPHY, J. (1978). Looking in classroom. New York: Harper & Row Publishers.

GRAHAM, G. (1973). The effects of a micro - teaching laboratory on the ability of teacher trainees to teach a novel skill to fifth and sixth grade children. Unpublished doctoral dissertation, University of Oregon.

GRAHAM, G. (1983). Review and implications of physical education experimental teaching unit research. In, T. Templin, & J. Olson (Eds), Teaching in Physical Education. Champaign: Human Kinetics, 244-253.

GRAHAM, G., & HEIMERER, E. (1981). Research on teacher effectiveness: a summary with implications for teaching. Quest, 33, 1, 14-25.

GRAHAM, G., SOARES, P., & HARRINGTON, W. (1983). Experienced teachers'effectiveness with intact classes: An ETU study. Journal of Teaching in Physical Education, 2, 2, 3-14.

GRIFFEY, D. (1983). ALT in context: on the non-linear and interactional characteristic of engaged time. In P. Dodds, & F. Rife (Eds), Time to learn in physical education: History, completed research, and potential future for Academic Learning Time in physical education, Monograph 1, 34-37.

GRIFFIN, P. (1980). Developing a systematic observation instrument to identify sex role dependent and sex role independent behavior among physical education teachers. Unpublished doctoral dissertation, University of Massachusetts.

References

GRIFFIN, P. (1983). "Gymnastics is a girl's thing": Student participation and interaction patterns in a middle school gymnastics unit. In, T. Templin, & J. Olson (Eds), Teaching in Physical Education. Champaign: Human Kinetics, 71-85.

GRIFFIN, P. (1984). Girls'Participation Patterns in a Middle School Team Sport Unit. Journal of Teaching Physical Education 4, 1, 30-38.

GRIFFIN, P. (1985). Boys'participation styles in a middle school physical education team sports unit. Journal of Teaching Physical Education, 4, 2, 100-110.

GUSTHART, L. (1983). Teaching behavior through five levels of field experiences. In, R. Telama, V. Varstala, J. Tiainen, L. Laakso, & T. Haajanen (Eds), Research in school physical education. Jyvaskyla: The foundation for promotion of physical culture and health, 328-335.

GUSTHART, L. (1985). Variations in Direct, Indirect, and Non-contributing Teacher Behavior. Journal of Teaching in Physical Education, 4, 2, 111-122.

GUSTHART, L., & RINK, J. (1983). Teaching behavior through various levels of field experiences. Journal of Teaching in physical education, 3, 1, 32-46.

HAMILTON, K. (1974). The effects of a competency - based intervention on student teacher and pupil behavior. Unpublished doctoral dissertation, Ohio State University.

HANKE, U. (1979). The importance of evaluation in modeling and feedback for the acquisition of teaching - skills. In, T. Tammivuori (Ed.), Evaluation. International congress of physical education, July 1976. Helsinki: Finnish society for research in sport and physical education, Publication 64, 74-80.

HARRINGTON, W. (1974). A study of feedback diversity in teaching physical education, Unpublished doctoral dissertation, University of Wisconsin.

References

HAWKINS, A., WIEGAND, R., & BAHNEMAN, C. (1983). The conceptual nature of ALT-PE and its use in an undergraduate teacher preparation program. In P. Dodds, & F. Rife (Eds), Time to learn in physical education: History, completed research, and potential future for Academic Learning Time in physical education, Monograph 1, 11-16.

HEINILA, L. (1979). Analyzing systems in the evaluation of the teacher - pupil interaction process in physical education classes. In, T. Tammivuori (Ed.), Evaluation. International congress of physical education, July 1976. Helsinki: Finnish society for research in sport and physical education, Publication 64, 37-58.

HEINILA, L. (1980). Developing a system (PEIAC/LH-75) for describing teacher-pupil interaction in physical education classes: objectivity and content validity of coding. In, G. Schillings, & W. Baur (Eds), Audiovisuelle Medien im Sport. Moyens audiovisuels dans le sport. Audiovisual means in sports. Basel, Birkhauser Verlag, 361-370.

HEINILA, L. (1983). Developing a system (PEIAC/LH-75) for describing teacher - pupil interaction in physical education classes: construct validity and sensitivity. In R. Telama, V. Varstala, J. Tiainen, L. Laakso & T. Haajanen. Research in school physical education. Jyvaskyla: The foundation for promotion of physical culture and health, 124-132.

HOFFMAN, S. (1983). Clinical diagnosis as a pedagogical skill. In, T. Templin, & J. Olson (Eds.), Teaching in Physical Education. Champaign: Human Kinetics, 35-45.

HOUGH, J.B. (1967). An observational system for the analysis of classroom instruction. In Amidon E., & Hough J.B., Interaction analysis: theory, research and application, Reading, Mass., Addison Wesley Pub. cy., 150-157.

HOULD, B., & BRUNELLE, J. (1981). Le temps de pratique pendant les périodes d'enseignement: un miroir de l'efficacité de la communication de l'instructeur. In, G. Bérubé (Ed.), Le Hockey municipal: défi des années 80., Québec, F.Q.H.G., 36-74.

References

HUGHLEY, C. (1973). Modification of teaching behavior in physical education. Unpublished doctoral dissertation, Ohio State University.

HUGHLEY, C. (1983). OSU Teacher Behavior Rating Scale. In, P. Darst, V. Mancini, & D. Zakrajsek (Eds), Systematic Observation Instrumentation for Physical Education. West Point: Leisure Press, 129-132.

HUPE, A. (1974). The development of a system for coding teacher behavior in physical education. Unpublished doctoral dissertation, Teachers College, Columbia University.

HURWITZ, D. (1983). Tearcher's Role in Providing Activity Choice (TRIPAC). In, P. Darst, V. Mancini, & D. Zakrajsek (Eds), Systematic Observation Instrumentation for Physical Education. West Point: Leisure Press, 218-241.

HURWITZ, R. (1974). A system to describe certain aspects of the physical education teacher's role in the learning - activity selection process. Unpublished doctoral dissertation, Teachers College, Columbia University.

HUTSLAR, S. (1976). The effects of training cooperating teachers in applied behavior analysis on student teaching behavior in physical education. Unpublished doctoral dissertation, Ohio State University.

IMWOLD, C. (1980). The relationship between teaching experience and performance error diagnosis of a gymnastic skill. Unpublished doctoral dissertation, University of Pittsburgh.

IMWOLD, C., & HOFFMAN, S. (1983). Visual recognition of a gymnastics skill by experienced and inexperienced instructors. Research for Exercise and Sport, 54, 149-155.

IMWOLD, C., RIDER, R., TWARDY, B., OLIVER, P., GRIFFIN, M., & ARSENAULT, D. (1984). The effect of Planning on the Teaching Behavior of Preservice Physical Education Teachers. Journal of Teaching in Physical Education, Vol. 4, 1, 50-56.

References

JACOBY, J. (1975). A comparison of the effects of command, reciprocal and individual styles of teaching on the development of selected sport skills. Unpublished doctoral dissertation, Ohio State University.

JOHNSON, T. (1983). Flow of Teacher Organizational Patterns (FOTOP). In, P. Darst, V. Mancini, & D. Zakrajsek (Eds), Systematic Observation Instrumentation for Physical Education. West Point: Leisure Press, 269-274.

KASSON, P. (1974). Teaching and coaching behaviors of physical educators. Unpublished doctoral dissertation, University of Wisconsin.

KEILTY, G. (1975). The effect of instruction and supervision in interaction analysis on the preparation of student teachers. Unpublished doctoral dissertation, Boston University.

LACY, A., & DARST, P. (1984). Evolution of a systematic observation system: the A.S.U. coaching observation instrument. Journal of Teaching in physical education, 1, 3, 59-66.

LACY, A., & DARST, P. (1985). Systematic Observation of Behaviors of Winning High School Head Football Coaches. Journal of Teaching in Physical Education, Vol. 4, 4, 256-270.

LANGSDORF, E. (1979). A systematic observation of football coaching behavior in a major University environment. Unpublished doctoral dissertation, Arizona State University.

LANGSDORF, E. (1983). Coaching Behavior Recording Form. In, P. Darst, V. Mancini, & D. Zakrajsek (Eds), Systematic Observation Instrumentation for Physical Education. West Point: Leisure Press, 306-315.

LAUBACH, S. (1975). The development of a system for coding student behavior in physical education classes. Unpublished doctoral dissertation, Teachers College, Columbia University.

LAUBACH, S. (1983). The BESTPED System. In, P. Darst, V. Mancini, & D. Zakrajsek (Eds), Systematic Observation Instrumentation for Physical Education. West Point: Leisure Press, 242-262.

LEVISON, M. (1978). A descriptive instrument to investigate teacher references to the task environment during the facilitation of perceptual motor skills. Unpublished doctoral dissertation, Teachers College, Columbia University.

LEWIN, K., LIPPITT, R., & WHITE, R.K. (1939). Patterns of aggressive behavior in experimentally created "social climates", J. Social Psychol., 10, 271-299.

LEWIS, G. (1974). The effects of training student teachers in the use of interaction analysis. Unpublished doctoral dissertation, Temple University.

LEWIS, K. (1979). The effects of interaction analysis on achieving verbal control of teaching styles in elementary physical education. Unpublished doctoral dissertation, University of Florida.

LEWIS, G. (1983). Individualized Teacher Behavior Analysis System (ITBAS). In, P. Darst, V. Mancini, & D. Zakrajsek (Eds), Systematic Observation Instrumentation for Physical Education. West Point: Leisure Press, 109-117.

LOCKE, L. (1977). Research on teaching physical education: new hope for a dismal science. Quest, 28, 2-16.

LOCKE, L. (1979). Supervision, schools and student teaching : Why things stay the same. In, G. Scott (Ed.), The Academy Papers, N°13. Washington, D.C. : The American Academy of Physical Education, 65-74.

LOCKE, L., & DODDS, P. (1984). Research on Teaching Teachers: Where Are We Now? Journal of Teaching in Physical Education, Monograph 2, 1-85.

LOCKE, L., & WOODS, S. (1982). Teacher enthusiasm ! Journal of Teaching in Physical Education, 1, 3, 3-14.

LOMBARDO, B. (1979). The observation and description of the teaching behavior and innteraction of selected physical education teachers. Unpublished doctoral dissertation, Boston University.

LOMBARDO, B. (1982). Variability in teaching behavior and interaction in the gym: a two-year analysis. In, M. Piéron, & J. Cheffers (Eds), Studying the teaching in physical education. Liège: AIESEP, 93-101.

LOMBARDO, B., FARAONE, N., & POTHIER, D. (1982). The behavior of youth sport coaches: a preliminary analysis. In, Piéron, M., & Cheffers, J. (Eds), Studying the teaching in physical education: AIESEP, 189-196.

LOMBARDO, B., & CHEFFERS, J. (1983). Variability in teaching behavior and interaction in the gymnasium. Journal of Teaching in Physical Education, 2, 2, 33-48.

LORD, M. (1981-82). A characterization of dance teacher behaviors techni-que and choreography classes. Dance research journal, 14, 1, & 2, 15-24.

LOVE, A., & RODERICK, J. (1983). Love - Roderick Categories of Teacher Non-Verbal Behavior System. In, P. Darst, V. Mancini, & D. Zakrajsek (Eds), Systematic Observation Instrumentation for Physical Education. West Point: Leisure Press, 53-57.

LUCAS, G. (1978a). Utilizing interaction analysis to specify interaction between pupils and teachers in conceptual approach physical education. In, M. Piéron (Ed.), Towards a science of teaching: Teaching analysis. Liège, A.I.E.S.E.P., 44-52.

LUCAS, G. (1978b). Teaching analysis by utilizing the Florida taxonomy of cognitive behavior for comparing traditional and conceptual physical education lessons in secondary grades. In, M. Piéron (Ed.), Towards a science of teaching: Teaching analysis. Liège: A.I.E.S.E.P., 89-97.

LUCAS, G. (1980). Coaching communication patterns. A pilot study utilizing methods for determining patterns of communication among Canadian College championships coaches. In, G. Schillings,

& W. Baur (Eds), Audiovisuelle Medien im Sport. Moyens audiovisuels dans le sport. Audiovisual means in sports. Basel,
Birkhauser Verlag,

LUCAS, G., READ, L. (1982). Reasons physical education is not
an activity subject. In, Piéron, M., & Cheffers, J. (Eds), Studying the teaching in physical education: AIESEP, 131-139.

LUNT, J. (1974). A Procedure for Systematically Describing
Teacher-Student Verbal and Nonverbal Interaction in the Teaching
of Choreography. Unpublished doctoral dissertation, University of
North Carolina of Greenboro.

LYDON, M. (1978). Decision - making in elementary school age
children: effects of a convergent curriculum model upon motor
skill development, self-concept and group interaction. Unpublished doctoral dissertation, Boston University.

LYDON, M., & CHEFFERS, J. (1984). Decision-Making in Elementary
School Age Children: Effects upon Motor Learning and Self-Concept
Development. Research Quarterly for Exercise and Sport, 55, 135-
140.

MANCINI, V. (1974). A comparison of two decision - making
models in an elementary human movement program based on attitudes
on interaction patterns. Unpublished doctoral dissertation,
Boston University.

MANCINI, V., CHEFFERS, J., & ZAICHKOWSKY, L. (1976). Decision-
making in Elementary Children: Effects on Attitudes and Interaction. Research Quarterly, 47, 80-85.

MANCINI, V., & AGNEW, M. (1978). An analysis of teaching and
coaching behaviors. In, W. Straub (Ed.), Sport psychology. An
analysis of athlete behaviors. Ithaca, N.Y.: Mouvement publications, 402-409.

MANCINI, V., & CHEFFERS, J. (1983). Cheffers'adaptation of the
Flanders'interaction analysis system II (CAFIAS II). In, P.
Darst, V. Mancini, & D. Zakrajsek (Eds), Systematic Observation
Instrumentation for Physical Education. West Point: Leisure
Press, 96-99.

MANCINI, V., WUEST, D., CLARK, E., & RIDOSH, N. (1983). A comparison of interaction patterns and academic learning time of low- and high-burnout secondary physical educators. In, T. Templin, & J. Olson (Eds), Teaching in Physical Education. Champaign: Human Kinetics, 197-208.

MANCUSO, J.T., (1972). The verbal and nonverbal interaction between secondary school physical education student teachers and their pupils. Unpublished doctoral dissertation, University of Illinois.

MANCUSO, J. (1983). The Mancuso adaptation for verbal and non-verbal behaviors. In, P. Darst, V. Mancini, & D. Zakrajsek (Eds), Systematic Observation Instrumentation for Physical Education. West Point: Leisure Press, 58-94.

MARTINEK, T. (1976). A comparison of the vertical and horizontal models of teaching in the development of specific motor skills and self-concept. Unpublished doctoral dissertation, Boston University.

MARTINEK, T. (1981). Physical Attractiveness: Effects on Teacher Expectations and Dyadic Interactions in Elementary Age Children. Journal of Sport Psychology, 3, 196-205.

MARTINEK, T. (1983). Creating Golem and Galatea effects during physical education instruction: A social psychological perspective. In T. Templin, & J. Olson (Eds), Teaching in Physical Education, Champaign: Human Kinetics, 59-70.

MARTINEK, T., CROWE, P., & REJESKI, W. (1982). Pygmalion in the Gym: Causes and Effects of Expectations in Teaching And Coaching. West Point, N.Y.: Leisure Press.

MARTINEK, T., & JOHNSON, S. (1979). Teacher expectations: effects on dyadic interactions and self concept in elementary age children. Research Quarterly, 50, 60-70.

MARTINEK, T., & KARPER, W. (1981). Teacher expectations for handicapped and non-handicapped children in mainstreamed physical education classes. Perceptual and motor skills, 53, 327-330.

References

MARTINEK, T., & KARPER, W. (1982). Canonical relationship among motor ability, expression of effort, teacher expectations and dyadic interactions in elementary age children. Journal of teaching in physical education, vol. 1, 2, 26-39.

MARTINEK, T., & KARPER, W. (1983). The influence of teacher expectations on ALT in physical education instruction. In P. Dodds, & F. Rife (Eds), Time to learn in physical education: History, completed research, and potential future for Academic Learning Time in physical education, Monograph 1, 48-52.

MARTINEK, T., & KARPER, W. (1984). Multivariate Relationships of Specific Impression Cues with Teacher Expectations and Dyadic Interactions in Elementary Physical Education Classes. Research Quarterly for Exercise and Sport, 55, 32-40.

MARTINEK, T., & MANCINI, V. (1983). The dyadic adaptation of the Cheffers'adaptation of the Flanders' interaction analysis system (DAC). In, P. Darst, V. Mancini, & D. Zakrajsek (Eds), Systematic Observation Instrumentation for Physical Education. West Point: Leisure Press, 100-105.

MARTINEK, T., ZAICHKOVSKY, L., & CHEFFERS, J. (1977). Decision-making in elementary age children: effects on motor skills and self-concept. Research Quarterly, 48, 349-357.

MAWDSLEY R. (1977). Comparison of teacher behaviors in regular and adapted movement classes. Unpublished doctoral dissertation, Boston University.

MAWER, M., & BROWN, G. (1982). Teacher guidance behaviour in educational gymnastics lessons with elementary age children. In, Piéron, M., & Cheffers, J. (Eds), Studying the teaching in physical education: AIESEP, 123-129.

MAWSON, L. (1973). An analysis of teaching patterns of the student teacher, cooperating teacher and supervising teacher during student teaching. Unpublished doctoral dissertation, University of Oregon.

McEWEN, T., & GRAHAM, G. (1982). Patterns of teaching behaviors employed by physical education teachers and skill learning time.

References

In, Piéron, M., & Cheffers, J. (Eds), Studying the teaching in physical education: AIESEP, 3-22.

McKENZIE, T. (1976). Development of a model behaviorally-based teacher training center for physical educators. Unpublished doctoral dissertation, Ohio State University.

McKENZIE, T. (1981). Modification, transfer and maintenance of the verbal behavior of an experienced physical education teacher: a single-subject analysis. Journal of Teaching in Physical Education, Introductory issue, 48-56.

McKENZIE, T. (1986). Analysis of the Practice Behavior of Elite Athletes. In, M. Piéron, & G. Graham (Ed.), The 1984 Olympic Scientific Congress Proceedings. Vol. 6, Sport Pedagogy. Champaign: Human Kinetics, 117-121.

McKENZIE, L. & RUSHALL, B. (1980). Controlling inappropriate behaviors in a competitive swimming environment. Education and Treatment of Children, 3, 205-216.

McLEISH, J. HOWE, B., & JACKSON, J. (1981). Effective teaching in physical education. Faculty of Education, University of Victoria, B.C.

McLEISH, J. (1985). An overall view. In, B.L. Howe, & J.J. Jackson (Eds), Teaching Effectiveness Research. Victoria, British Columbia: University of Victoria, 1985.

MELOGRANO, V. (1971). Effects of teacher personality, teacher choice of educational objectives and teacher behavior on student achievement. Unpublished doctoral dissertation, Temple University.

MELOGRANO, V. (1983). A modification of the Flanders interaction analysis system. In, P. Darst, V. Mancini, & D. Zakrajzek (Eds), Systematic Observation Instrumentation for Physical Education. West Point: Leisure Press, 34-40.

MERTLER, C. (1974). The use of behavior modification techniques in a sport environment. Unpublished doctoral dissertation, Ohio State University.

References

METZLER, M. (1979). The measurement of academic learning time in physical education. Unpublished doctoral dissertation, Ohio State University.

METZLER, M. (1982). Adapting the academic learning time instructional model to physical education teaching. Journal of teaching in physical education. Vol. 1, 2, 44-55.

METZLER, M.(1983a). Using academic learning time in process-product studies with experimental teaching units. In, T. Templin, & J. Olson (Eds), Teaching in Physical Education, Champaign: Human Kinetics, 185-196.

METZLER, M. (1983b). An interval recording system for measuring academic learning time in physical education. In, P. Darst, V. Mancini, & D. Zakrajsek (Eds), Systematic Observation Instrumentation for Physical Education. West Point: Leisure Press, 181-195.

METZLER, M. (1983c). ALT-PE for inservice teachers: questions and insights. In P. Dodds, & F. Rife (Eds), Time to learn in physical education: History, completed research, and potential future for Academic Learning Time in physical education, Monograph 1, 17-21.

METZLER, M. (1986). Analysis of a Mastery Learning/Personalized System of Instruction for Teaching Tennis. In, M. Piéron, & G. Graham (Ed.), The 1984 Olympic Scientific Congress Proceedings. Vol. 6, Sport Pedagogy. Champaign: Human Kinetics, 63-70.

MITZEL, H. (1960). Teacher effectiveness, In, C. Harris (Ed), Encyclopedia of education research (3rd Ed.), New York: Mc Millan.

MORGENEGG, B., (1978a). The pedagogical functions of physical education teachers. Unpublished doctoral dissertation, Teachers College, Columbia University.

MORGENEGG, B. (1978b). Pedagogical moves. In, W. Anderson, & G. Barrette (Eds), What'going on in gym: descriptive studies of physical education classes. Mongograph 1, Motor skills: theory into practice, 63-74.

References

MORGENEGG, B. (1983). Instrument for the analysis of the pedagogical functions of physical education teachers (PEDFUNC). In,
P. Darst, V. Mancini, & D. Zakrajsek (Eds), Systematic Observation Instrumentation for Physical Education. West Point: Leisure
Press, 200-217.

NYGAARD, G. (1971). An analysis of verbal interaction in physical education classes. Unpublished doctoral dissertation, University Oregon.

NYGAARD, G. (1975). Interaction analysis in physical education
classes. Research Quarterly, 46, 351-357.

NYGAARD, G. (1978). Three research papers on the analysis of
teaching in physical education. In, M. Piéron (Ed), Towards a
science of teaching physical education: teaching analysis. Liège:
AIESEP, 53-58.

OIEN, F. (1979). Teacher behavior directed towards individual
students in physical education classes. Unpublished doctoral
dissertation, University of Massachusetts.

OLSON, J. (1979). Adaptation of the observational system for
instructional analysis (O.S.I.A.) for use in physical education.
Unpublished doctoral dissertation, Ohio State University.

OLSON, J. (1982). CATENAS: A probe for relevant instructional
configurations in physical education settings. In, Piéron, M., &
Cheffers, J. (Eds), Studying the teaching in physical education:
AIESEP, 113-122.

OLSON, J. (1983a). The observational system for instructional
analysis for use in physical education (OSIA-PE). In, P. Darst,
V. Mancini, & D. Zakrajsek (Eds), Systematic Observation Instrumentation for Physical Education. West Point: Leisure Press, 168-
186.

OLSON, J. (1983b). Catenas: Exploring meaning. In, T. Templin,
& J. Olson (Eds), Teaching in Physical Education. Champaign:
Human Kinetics, 286-297.

References

OSPELT, R., & SCHILLING, G. (1978). Le comportement du maître dans l'enseignement du sport. Jeunesse et sport, 35, 194-204.

O'SULLIVAN, M. (1983). The effects of inservice education on the teaching effectiveness of experienced physical educators. Unpublished doctoral dissertation, Ohio State University.

O'SULLIVAN, M. (1985). A descriptive analytical study of student teacher effectiveness and student behaviour in secondary school physical education. In, B.L. Howe , & J.J. Jackson (Eds), Teaching Effectiveness Research. Victoria, British Columbia: University of Victoria, 1985.

PAESE, P. (1986). Comparison of Teacher Behavior and Criterion Process Variables in an Experimental Teaching Unit (ETU) Taught by Preservice Physical Education Majors at the Entrance and Exit Levels. In, M. Piéron, & G. Graham (Ed.), The 1984 Olympic Scientific Congress Proceedings. Vol. 6, Sport Pedagogy. Champaign: Human Kinetics, 71-76.

PARE, C., LIRETTE, M., & CARON, F. (1983). L'analyse du temps de pratique active chez des élèves du secteur adaptation scolaire. Revue des sciences de l'éducation. 9, 3, 401-417.

PARKER, M., & O'SULLIVAN, M. (1983). Modifying ALT-PE for game play contexts and other reflexions. In P. Dodds, & F. Rife (Eds), Time to learn in physical education: History, completed research, and potential future for Academic Learning Time in physical education, Monograph 1, 8-10.

PETERSEN, G., Curriculum, Teacher behavior patterns and student performance in physical education. Unpublished doctoral dissertation, Arizona State University, 1980.

PHILLIPS, D.,& CARLISLE, C. (1983a). The physical education teacher assessment instrument. Journal of Teaching in Physical Education, vol. 2, 2, 62-76.

PHILLIPS, D., & CARLISLE, C. (1983b). A comparison of physical education teachers categorized as most and least effective. Journal of Teaching in Physical Education, vol. 2, 55-67.

References

PIERON, M. (1976). Didactique et méthodologie des activités physiques. Liège: Université de Liège.

PIERON, M. (1978a). Pédagogie rénovée des activités physiques. In, Landry F., & Orban W.A.R., International congress of physical activity sciences, 7. Motor learning, sport psychology, pedagogy and didactics of physical activity. Miami, Symposia specialists, 383-391.

PIERON, M. (1978b). Variation du comportement verbal d'ensei-gnants selon la spécialité sportive enseignée. In, Landry F., & Orban W.A.R., International congress of physical activity scien-ces, 7. Motor learning, sport psychology, pedagogy and didactics of physical activity. Miami, Symposia specialists, 443-449.

PIERON, M. (1980). L'analyse de l'enseignement des activités physiques. Résultats, tendances, perspectives. In, G. Schillings, & W. Baur (Eds), Audiovisuelle Medien im Sport. Moyens audio-visuels dans le sport. Audiovisual means in sports. Basel, Birk-hauser Verlag, 324-336.

PIERON, M. (1982a). Analyse de l'enseignement des activités physiques. Bruxelles: Ministère de l'Education Nationale et de la Culture Française.

PIERON, M. (1982b). Behaviors of low and high achievers in physical education classes. In, Piéron, M., & Cheffers, J. (Eds), Studying the teaching in physical education: AIESEP, 53-60.

PIERON, M. (1982c). Effectiveness of teaching a psycho-motor task. Study in a micro-teaching setting. In, M. Piéron, & J. Cheffers (Eds), Studying the Teaching in Physical Education. Liège: A.I.E.S.E.P., 79-89.

PIERON, M. (1983a). Teacher and pupil behavior and the inter-action process in physical education classes. In R. Telama, V. Varstala, J. Tiainen, L. Laakso, & T. Haajanen. Research in school physical education. Jyvaskyla: The foundation for promo-tion of physical culture and health, 13-30.

PIERON, M. (1983b). Effectiveness of teaching a psychomotor task (Gymnastic routine). Study in a class setting. In, R.

References

Telama, V. Varstala, J. Tiainen, L. Laakso, & T. Haajanen (Eds), Research in school physical education. Jyvaskyla: The foundation for promotion of physical culture and health, 222-227.

PIERON, M. (1986). Analysis of the Research Based on Observation of the Teaching of Physical Education. In, M. Piéron, & G. Graham (Ed.), The 1984 Olympic Scientific Congress Proceedings. Vol. 6, Sport Pedagogy. Champaign: Human Kinetics, 193-202.

PIERON, M., & CLOES, M. (1981). Interactions between teachers and students in selected sports activities: the student as a starting point. Artus (Rio de Janeiro), 9/11, 185-188.

PIERON, M., &, DELMELLE, R. (1981). Descriptive study of Teacher's Feedback in two educational situations. Artus (Rio de Janeiro), 9/11, 193-196.

PIERON, M., & DELMELLE, R. (1982). Agumented feedback in teaching physical education: Responses from the students. In, Piéron, M., & Cheffers, J. (Eds), Studying the teaching in physical education: AIESEP, 141-150.

PIERON, M., & DELMELLE, R. (1983). Le retour d'information dans l'enseignement des activités physiques. Motricité Humaine, 1, 12-17.

PIERON, M., & DELMELLE, V. (1983). Les réactions à la prestation de l'élève. Etude dans l'enseignement de la danse moderne. Revue de l'éducation physique, 23, 4, 35-41.

PIERON, M., & DEVILLERS, C. (1980). Multidimensional analysis of informative feedback in teaching physical activities. In, G. Schilling, & W. Baur (Eds), Audiovisuelle Medien im Sport. Moyens audiovisuels dans le sport. Audiovisual means in sports, Basel: Birkhauser Verlag, 277-284.

PIERON, M., & DOHOGNE, A. (1980). Comportements des élèves dans des classes d'éducation physique conduites par des enseignants en formation. Revue de l'Education Physique, 20, 4, 11-18.

PIERON, M., & DRION, C. (1977). Analyse de l'interaction entre le professeur et ses élèves en éducation physique, par le système

References

de Hough. Revue de l'Education Physique. 17, 27-37.

PIERON, M., & FORCEILLE, C. (1983). Observation du comportement des élèves dans des classes de l'enseignement secondaire: influence de leur niveau d'habileté. Revue de l'Education Physique, 23, 2, 9-16.

PIERON, M., & GEORIS, A.M. (1983). Comportements d'enseignants et interactions avec leurs élèves, observation dans l'enseignement de la "modern dance". Revue de l'Education Physique, 23, 4, 42-45.

PIERON, M., & GRAHAM, G. (1984). Research on Physical Education Teacher Effectiveness: The Experimental Teaching Units, International Journal of Physical Education, 21, 3, 9-14.

PIERON, M., & HACOURT, J. (1979). Teaching behaviours at different levels of physical education teaching. Bulletin of the "Fédération Internationale d'Education Physique", 49, 2, 33-41.

PIERON, M., & HAAN, J.M. (1980). Pupils activities, time on task and behaviours in high school physical education teaching. Bulletin of the Fédération Internationale d'Education Physique, 50, 3/4, 62-68.

PIERON, M., & HAAN, J.M. (1981). Interactions between teacher and students in a physical education setting. Observation of students behaviours. In, Haag, & coll. (Eds), Sport, Erziehung und Evaluation. Physical Education and Evaluation. Proceedings of the XXII ICHPER World Congress, Kiel, July 23-27, 1979. Schorndorf, Verlag Karl Hoffmann, 364-368.

PIERON, M., NETO, C., CARREIRO DA COSTA, F. (1985). La rétro-action (feedback) dans des situations d'enseignement en gymnastique et en basket-ball, Motricidade Humana, 1, 25-33.

PIERON, M., & PIRON, J. (1981). Recherche de critères d'efficacité de l'enseignement d'habiletés motrices. Sport, 24, 144-161.

PLACEK, J., & RANDALL, L. (1986). Comparison of Academic Learning Time in Physical Education: Students of Specialists and Non specialists. Journal of Teaching in Physical Education, 5, 157-165.

QUARTERMAN, J. (1978). A descriptive analysis of teaching physical education in the elementary schools. Unpublished doctoral dissertation, Ohio State University.

QUARTERMAN, J. (1983). Physical education teacher/coach observational system. In, P. Darst, V. Mancini, & D. Zakrajsek (Eds), Systematic Observation Instrumentation for Physical Education. West Point: Leisure Press, 300-305.

RANKIN, K. (1975). Verbal and non-verbal interaction analysis of student teachers with students in elementary physical education. Unpublished doctoral dissertation, University Kansas.

RANKIN, K. (1983). The Rankin Interaction analysis system (RIAS). In, P. Darst, V. Mancini, & D. Zakrajsek (Eds), Systematic Observation Instrumentation for Physical Education. West Point: Leisure Press, 65-69.

RATE, R. (1980). A descriptive analysis of academic learning time and coaching behaviors in interscholastic athletic practices. Unpublished doctoral dissertation, Ohio State University.

REESE, R. (1983). The effects of joint supervision on the teaching effectiveness of elementary physical education student teachers. Unpublished doctoral dissertation, Ohio State University.

REHBEIN, E. (1981). An approach to a multi-dimensional analysis of verbal and non-verbal teacher behaviour in physical education classes. In H. Haag & al. (Eds), Physical education and evaluation. Proceedings of the XXII ICHPER World Congress, Kiel, July 23-27, 1979. Schorndorf: Hoffmann Verlag, 333-340.

REPONEN, P. (1979). Personality and teaching behavior of physical educa-tion students. In, T. Tammivuori (Ed.), Evaluation. International congress of physical education, July 1976. Helsinki, Finnish society for research in sport and physical education, Publication nr 64, 1979, 96-115.

References

RIFE, F. (1973). Modification of student-teacher behavior and its effects on pupil behavior. Unpublished doctoral dissertation, Ohio State University.

RIFE, F., SHUTE, S., & DODDS, P. (1985). ALT-PE Versions I and II: Evolution of a Student-Centered Observation System in Physical Education. Journal of Teaching in Physical Education, Vol. 4, 2, 134-142.

RIFE, F., & DODDS, P. (1978). Developing evidential bases for educational practice through the single subject research paradigm. Motor skills: theory into practice, 3, 1, 40-48.

RIFE, F., SHUTE, S., & DODDS, P. (1985). ALT-PE Version I and II evolution of a student-centered observation system in physical education, 4, 134-142.

RINK, J. (1979). Development of systems for the observation for content development in physical education. Unpublished doctoral dissertation, Ohio State University.

RINK, J. (1983). The stability of teaching behavior over a unit of instruction. In, T. Templin, & J. Olson (Eds), Teaching in Physical Education. Champaign: Human Kinetics, 318-328.

RITSON, R., SMITH, R., & TWA, H. (1982). Student and teacher interaction analysis: a comparison of activities, age groups and sex of the students in physical education. Journal of teaching in physical education, 1, 2, 15-25.

ROLIDER, A. (1979). Effects of enthusiasm training on subsequent teacher behavior. Unpublished doctoral dissertation, Ohio State University.

ROLIDER, A., SIEDENTOP, D., & VAN HOUTEN, R. (1984). Effects of enthusiasm training on subsequent teacher enthousiastic behavior. Journal of Teaching in physical education, 3, 2, 47-59.

ROSENSHINE, B.V. (1978). Academic engaged time, content covered, and direct instruction. Journal of Education (Boston), 160, 3, 38-66.

References

ROSENSHINE, B. (1980). How time is spent in elementary class-room. In, Denham C., & Liebermann A. (Eds), Time to learn. Washington, National Institute of Education, 107-126.

ROSENSHINE, B., & FURST, N. (1973). The use of direct observation to study teaching. In, R. Travers (Ed), Second Handbook of research on teaching. Chicago, Rand Mc Nally, 122-183.

RUSHALL, B. (1975a). Behavior patterns of coaches and athletes: a preliminary study. In, Trabajos cientificos. III Congreso Mundial de la Sociedad Internacional de Psychologie del Deporte. Madrid: INEF, vol. 2, 313-329.

RUSHALL, B. (1975b). Applied behavior analysis for sports and physical education. International Journal of Sports Psychology, 6, 2, 75-88.

RUSHALL, B. (1982). What coaches do: Behavioral Evidence of Coaching Effectiveness. In, L. Wankel & R. Wilberg (Eds), Psychology of sport and motor behavior: Research and Practice. Proceedings of the CSPLSP Annual Meeting. Edmonton, AL: CSPLSP, 185-202.

RUSHALL, B. (1983). Teacher / coach and pupil athlete observation schedules. In, P. Darst, V. Mancini, & D. Zakrajsek (Eds), Systematic Observation Instrumentation for Physical Education. West Point: Leisure Press, 316-328.

RUSHALL, B., & Mc EACHERN, J. (1977). The effects of systematic behavioural feedback on teaching behaviours of physical education teachers. Canadian Journal of applied sport science, 2, 161-169.

RUSHALL, B., & RICHARDS, A. (1981). Teacher and class behaviors in physical education settings. Journal of Teaching in Physical Education, Introductory Issue, 39-47.

RUSHALL, B., & SIEDENTOP, D. (1972). The development of behavior in physical education. Philadelphia: Lea, & Febiger.

RUSHALL, B., & SMITH, K. (1979). The modification of the quality and quantity of behavior categories in a swimming coach. Journal of sports psychology, 1, 2, 138-150.

References

RYANS, D. (1960). Characteristics of teachers. Their Description, Comparison and Appraisal. A research study. Washington, D.C.: American Council on Education.

SALTER, W., & GRAHAM, G. (1985). The Effects of Three Disparate Instructional Approaches on Skill Attempts and Student Learning in an Experimental Teaching Unit. Journal of Teaching in Physical Education, Vol. 4, 3, 212-218.

SAMPH, T. (1968). Observer effects on teacher behavior. Unpublished doctoral dissertation, University Michigan.

SAUNDERS, J. (1981). Changes in the teaching behaviours of preservice teachers of movement / physical education in association with a micro-teaching course. In, H. Haag, & al. (Eds), Physical education and evaluation. Proceedings of the XXII ICHPER World Congress, Kiel, July 23-27, 1979. Schorndorf: Hoffmann Verlag, 340-345.

SCHEMPP, P. (1982). Enhancing creativity through children making decisions. In, Piéron, M., & Cheffers, J. (Eds), Studying the teaching in physical education: AIESEP, 161-165.

SCHEMPP, P. (1985). Becoming a Better Teacher: An Analysis of the Student Teaching Experience. Journal of Teaching in Physical Education, Vol.4, 3, 158-166.

SCHEMPP, P. (1986). Interaction Change as a Function of Grade Level in Physical Education. In, M. Piéron, & G. Graham (Ed.), The 1984 Olympic Scientific Congress Proceedings. Vol. 6, Sport Pedagogy. Champaign: Human Kinetics, 85-89.

SCHEMPP, P., CHEFFERS, J. ZAICHKOWSKY, L. (1983). Influence of decision-making on attitudes, creativity, motor skills, and self-concept in elementary children. Research Quarterly for Exercise and Sport, 53, 183-189.

SHUTE, S., DODDS, P., PLACEK, J., RIFE, F., & SILVERMAN, S. (1982). Academic Learning Time in elementary school movement education: a descriptive analytic study. Journal of Teaching in Physical Education, 1, 2, 3-14.

References

SHOWERS, J. (1974). A conceptual system for identifying teacher behaviors in physical education activity classes. Unpublished doctoral dissertation, University of North Carolina at Greensboro.

SIEDENTOP, D. (1976). Physical education. Introductory analysis. Dubuque: Wm C. Brown.

SIEDENTOP, D. (1981). The Ohio State University supervision research program summary report. Journal of Teaching in Physical Education, Introductory Issue, 30-38.

SIEDENTOP, D. (1983a). Developing teaching skills in physical education (2d Ed), Palo Alto: Mayfield Pub. Cy.

SIEDENTOP, D. (1983b). Academic Learning Time: Reflexions and prospects. In P. Dodds, & F. Rife (Eds), Time to learn in physical education: History, completed research, and potential future for Academic Learning Time in physical education, Monograph 1, 3-7.

SIEDENTOP, D., BIRDWELL, D., & METZLER, M. (1979). A process approach to measuring teaching effectiveness in physical education. Paper delivered at the AAHPERD research symposium. New Orleans.

SIEDENTOP, D., & RIFE, F. (1983). Data collection for managerial efficiency in physical education (DACOME-PE). In, P. Darst, V. Mancini, & D. Zakrajsek (Eds), Systematic Observation Instrumentation for Physical Education. West Point: Leisure Press, 133-139.

SIEDENTOP, D., TOUSIGNANT, M., & PARKER, M. (1982). Academic Learning Time - Physical Education, 1982 Revision, Coding Manual. Ohio State University.

SILVERMAN, S. (1983). The student as the unit of analysis: Effect on descriptive data and process-outcome relationships in physical education. In, T. Templin, & J. Olson (Eds), Teaching in Physical Education. Champaign: Human Kinetics, 277-285.

References

SILVERMAN, S. (1985a). Student Characteristics Mediating Engagement-Outcome Relationships in Physical Education. Research Quarterly for Exercise and Sport, 56, 66-72.

SILVERMAN, S. (1985b). Relationship of Engagement and Practice Trials to Student Achievement. Journal of Teaching in Physical Education, Vol. 5, 1, 13-21.

SILVERMAN, S., DODDS, P., PLACEK, J. SHUTE, S., & RIFE, F. (1984). Academic Learning Time in elementary school physical education (ALT-PE) for student subgroups and instructional activity units. Research Quarterly for Exercise and Sport. 55, 365-370.

SIMON, A., & BOYER, E. (1970). Mirrors for Behaviors. Philadelphia: Research for Better Schools.

SINGER, R., & DICK, W. (1974). Teaching physical education. A systems approach. Boston: Houghton Mifflin.

SMITH, R., SMOLL, B., & CURTIS, B. (1979). Coach effectiveness training: a cognitive - behavioral approach to enhancing relationship skills in youth sport coaches. Journal of Sport Psychology, 1, 59-75.

SMITH, R., SMOLL, F., & HUNT, E. (1977). A system for the behavioral assessment of athletic coaches. Research Quarterly, 48, 401-407.

SMOLL, F., SMITH, R., CURTIS, B., & HUNT, E. (1978). Toward a mediational model of coach-player relationship. Research Quarterly, 49, 528-541.

SOAR, R. (1973). Follow through classroom process measurement and pupil growth (1970-71) final report. Gainesville, Fla: University of Florida (ERIC Document Reproduction Service N° ED 106297.

SOLOMON, D. & KENDALL, A. Individual characteristics and children's performance in varied educational settings. Rockville, MD: Montgomery County Public Schools (cited by Rosenshine, 1976).

References

SPALANZANI, C., BRUNELLE, J., & TREMPE, L. (1981). Analyse du climat créé par des entraîneurs de hockey pendant des tournois. In, Bérube G. (Ed.), Le hockey municipal: défi des années 80. Québec: Féfération de hockey sur glace, 76-104.

SPLINTER, P., TAVECCHIO, L., KEMPER, H., RAS, J., SNEL, J., & VERSCHUUR, R. (1979). A physical education interaction analysis system - Sensibility of the categories to teaching styles. In, T. Tammivuori (Ed.), Evaluation. International congress of physical education, July 1976. Helsinki, Finnish society for research in sport and physical education, Publication nr 64, 69-74.

SPLINTER, P., & coll. (Undated). Observation of teaching beha-viour in physical education with the physical education inter-action analysis system (PEIAS). Experimental research and explo-rations with respect to reliability and construct validity of categories. Unpublished doctoral dissertation, University of Amsterdam.

STALLINGS, J., & KASKOWITZ, D. (1974). Follow through classroom evaluation 1972-1973. Menlo Park, CA: Stanford research insti-tute.

STEWART, M. (1977). A descriptive analysis of teaching beha-viors and its relationships to presage and context variables. Unpublished doctoral dissertation Ohio State University.

STEWART, M. (1983). Observational recording record of physical educator's teaching behavior (ORRPETB). In, P. Darst, V. Mancini, & D. Zakrajsek (Eds), Systematic Observation Instrumentation for Physical Education. West Point: Leisure Press, 155-167.

TAVECCHIO, L., SPLINTER, P., KEMPER, H., RAS, K., SNEL, J., VERSCHUUR, R. (1977). Development and application of a physical education interaction analysis system. International Journal of Physical Education, 14, 12-18.

TAYLOR, J. (1979). Development of the physical education obser-vation instrument using generalizability study theory. Research Quarterly, 50, 468-481.

References

TELAMA, R., VARSTALA, V., HEIKINARO-JOHANSSON, P., & PAUKKU, P. (1986). Relationship Between Pupils' Leisure-Time Physical Activity and Motor Behavior During Physical Education Lessons. In, M. Piéron, & G. Graham (Ed.), The 1984 Olympic Scientific Congress Proceedings. Vol. 6, Sport Pedagogy. Champaign: Human Kinetics, 57-62.

TELAMA, R., PAUKKU, P., VARSTALA, V., & PAANANEN, M. (1982). Pupil's physical activity and learning behaviour in physical education classes. In, M. Piéron, & J. Cheffers (Eds), Studying the teaching in physical education. Liège: AIESEP, 23-35.

TELAMA, R., VARSTALA, V., PAUKKU, P., PAANANEN, M., & HEIKINARO-JOHANSSON, P. (1985). Pupils' learning behaviors and activity models in team sport lessons from pedagogical point of view. In, Teaching Team Sports International Congress. Roma: CONI-Scuola dello Sport, 256-272.

TEMPLIN, T. (1983). Triangulating ALT-PE: A research consideration. In P. Dodds, & F. Rife (Eds), Time to learn in physical education: History, completed research, and potential future for Academic Learning Time in physical education, Monograph 1, 38-41.

THARP, R., & GALLIMORE, R. (1976). What a coach can teach a teacher. Psychology today, Jan.

TIMER, M. (1983). A technique for observable verbal and non-verbal teacher-student interaction analysis (The Timer - Love adaptation of Flanders' interaction analysis system. In, P. Darst, V. Mancini, & D. Zakrajsek (Eds), Systematic Observation Instrumentation for Physical Education. West Point: Leisure Press, 41-52.

TOBEY, C. (1977). A descriptive analysis of the occurence of augmented feedback in physical education classes. Unpublished doctoral dissertation, Teachers College, Columbia University.

TOUSIGNANT, M. (1982). Analysis of the task structures in secondary physical education classes. Unpublished doctoral dissertation, Ohio State University.

References

TOUSIGNANT, M., & BRUNELLE, J. (1982a). What we have learned from students and how we can use it to improve curriculum and teaching. In, M. Piéron, & J. Cheffers (Eds), Studying the Teaching in Physical Education. Liège: A.I.E.S.E.P., 3-22.

TOUSIGNANT, M., BRUNELLE, J., PIERON, M., & DHILLON, G. (1983). What's happening to the AT-PE research outside the USA ? In P. Dodds, & F. Rife (Eds), Time to learn in physical education: History, completed research, and potential future for Academic Learning Time in physical education, Monograph 1, 27-33.

TWA, H. (1979). A comparison of male and female physical education teachers verbal and non verbal interaction at the elementary school level. Unpublished doctoral dissertation, University Oregon.

UNDERWOOD, G. (1978). An investigation into the teaching of a basketball lesson using interaction analysis techniques. In, M. Piéron (Ed.), Towards a science of teaching: Teaching analysis. Liège: A.I.E.S.E.P., 77-88.

UNDERWOOD, G. (1979). The use of interaction analysis and video tape recording in studying teaching behavior in physical education. In, T. Tammivuori (Ed.), Evaluation. International congress of physical education, July 1976. Helsinki, Finnish society for research in sport and physical education, Publication nr 64, 59-69.

UNDERWOOD, G. (1980). A comparison of direct and problem - solving approaches in the teaching of physical education. In, G. Schillings, & W. Baur (Eds), Audiovisuelle Medien im Sport. Moyens audiovisuels dans le sport. Audiovisual means in sports. Basel, Birkhauser Verlag, 285-296.

VARSTALA, V., PAUKKU, P., & TELAMA, R. (1983). Teacher and pupil behavior in P.E. classes. In R. Telama, V. Varstala, J. Tiainen, L. Laakso, & T. Haajanen. Research in school physical education. Jyvaskyla: The foundation for promotion of physical culture and health, 47-57.

VARSTALA, V., TELAMA, R., & AKKANEN, O. (1981). Teacher and student activities during physical education lessons. In H. Haag,

& al. (Eds), Physical education and evaluation. Proceedings of the XXII ICHPER World Congress, Kiel July 23-27, 1979. Schorndorf: Hoffmann Verlag, 368-374.

VAN DER MARS, H. (1984). The effects of periodic prompting on selected teaching behaviors of physical education student teachers. Unpublished doctoral dissertation. Ohio State University.

VAN DER MARS, H., MANCINI, V., & FRYE, P. (1981). Effects of interaction analysis training on perceived and observed teaching behaviors. Journal of Teaching in Physical Education, Introductory Issue, 57-65.

VENDIEN, C. (1981). A look at teachers behaviours: an objective analysis. In, H. Haag, et al. (Eds), Physical education and evaluation. Proceedings of the XXII ICHPER World Congress, Kiel, July 23-27, 1979. Schorndorf: Hoffmann Verlag, 345-350.

WESTCOTT, W. (1981). The supervising teacher: key role-model and change agent for teacher behavior. Motor skills: Theory into practice, 5, 2, 135-140.

WUEST, D., CHEFFERS, J., CHAMPION, L., & ZAICHKOWSKY, L. (1982). Multidimensional analysis of teaching. In, Piéron, M., & Cheffers, J. (Eds), Studying the teaching in physical education: AIESEP, 103-111.

WUEST, D., MANCINI, V., VAN DER MARS, H., & TERRILLION, K. (1986). The Academic Learning Time-Physical Education of High-, Average-, and Low-Skilled Female Intercollegiate Volleyball Players. In, M. Piéron, & G. Graham (Ed.), The 1984 Olympic Scientific Congress Proceedings. Vol. 6, Sport Pedagogy. Champaign: Human Kinetics, 123-129.

YERG, B. (1977). Relationships between teacher behaviors and pupil achievement in the psychomotor domain. Unpublished doctoral dissertation, University of Pittsburgh.

YERG, B. (1981a). The impact of selected presage and process behaviors on the refinement of a motor skill. Journal of teaching in physical education, 1, 1, 38-46.

References

YERG, B. (1981b). Reflections on the use of the RTE model in physical education. Research Quarterly for exercise and sport, 52, 38-47.

YERG, B. (1983). Re-examining the process - product paradigm for research on teaching effectiveness in physical education. In, T. Templin, & J. Olson (Eds), Teaching in Physical Education. Champaign: Human Kinetics, 310-317.

YERG, B., & TWARDY, B. (1982). Relationship of specified instructional teacher behaviors to pupil gain on a motor skill task. In, M. Piéron & J. Cheffers (Eds), Studying the Teaching in Physical Education. Liège, A.I.E.S.E.P., 61-68.

YOKOYAMA, J. (1981). A study of sport pedagogy as science for the practice of physical education instruction - As shown through the example of teachers verbal communication analysis. In, H. Haag, & al. (Eds), Physical education and evaluation. Proceedings of the XXII ICHPER World Congress, Kiel, July 23-27, 1979, Schorndorf: Hoffmann Verlag, 351-355.

ZAKRAJSEK, D.B. (1974). Patterns of instructional time utilization and relation teacher characteristics for seventh grade physical education in selected school, Ph. D., Kent State Univ.

ZAKRAJSEK, D. (1983). Pattern analysis. In, P. Darst, V. Mancini, & D. Zakrajsek (Eds), Systematic Observation Instrumentation for Physical Education. West Point: Leisure Press, 263-268.

ZEICHNER, K. (1980). Myths and realities: Field based experiences in preservice teacher education. Journal of Teacher Education, 31(6), 45-55.

NAME INDEX

241

SUBJECT INDEX